T0171648

Creating Balance in a World of STRESS

Six Key Habits to Avoid in order to Reduce Stress

Susan J. Del Gatto

Creating Balance in a World of STRESS
Six Key Habits to Avoid in order to Reduce Stress

iUniverse books may be ordered through booksellers or by contacting:

iUniverse
1663 Liberty Drive
Bloomington, IN 47403
www.iuniverse.com
1-800-Authors (1-800-288-4677)

Because of the dynamic nature of the Internet, any Web addresses or links contained in this book may have changed since publication and may no longer be valid.

ISBN: 978-1-4401-4905-4 (sc)
ISBN: 978-1-4401-4903-0 (hc)
ISBN: 978-1-4401-4904-7 (e)

Print information available on the last page.

iUniverse rev. date: 10/08/2015

This book is dedicated to you,
My extended family,
To help you in reaching your goals in life.

CONTENTS

PREFACE

Self improvement is something we choose to do when one day we look in the mirror and say, "I want to learn how to be a better person." "I want to take control of my life." "I want to display traits that others find uplifting and complementary." Well anyway, that's how it happened to me. I saw things in others that I knew I didn't like and I seen those same things in me. This is when I knew I didn't like myself the way I was, I wanted more out of life.

How I became successful at this is explained in depth throughout this book but in short, I looked where everyone looks when they are eager to learn and change, to others. I knew what characteristics and values I liked when I seen them in someone I admired and I knew I wanted to be happier. I also knew that for the most part, I always would dwell on negative thoughts and this certainly did not contribute to any happiness, it was more like depression. So I took what I knew, and for the next 28 years I researched what made people unhappy and how this could be reversed and of course, I used myself as the test subject.

Soul searching became my obsession. The first thing that I learned was about positive thinking and positive perception. I learned that positive thinking is not a natural gift it is a learned process of thought. This takes time, determination and most importantly, the willingness to not fall prey to the negativity that surrounds you. I chose two improvements that I wanted to make in my life and placed all of my focus on continuously practicing these behaviors. Once they became natural to me, I moved on to new improvements I wanted to make. This began to snowball.

If you could envision me filling a jar with marbles, and every marble represented an improvement, it would go something like this. With my first successful improvement one marble went into the jar but then another followed as this first change built my confidence, so I doubled my positive change. The second improvement four marbles dropped in the jar, the third eight marbles dropped in the jar. As I accepted the positive changes in my life they always created more positive changes. With all of the positive changes, there became no room in my life for the negative.

My other strong focus became directed towards stress since this seemed to be the culprit of many negative thought patterns as was fear. I accumulated thousands of hours of knowledge while feeding my hunger on this subject. You could tell my sharp interest in these topics through college since the only courses I received straight A's in from day one to the end was psychology. I took the other classes just because they insisted.

My obsession turned into my passion to share the knowledge of these topics with others who seek to find inner happiness and outer success. Now, after all of this research, observation, self analysis, and somewhere between thousands and hundreds of thousands of hours of thought, interpretation and trial and error, I would like to bypass my errors and share my successes to give you a shortcut. This plan describes the key elements to follow which will empower you to find inner peace, happiness and success in your journey through life. You will love the way you feel with no more self doubt, no more worry, no more fear or feeling helpless, insecure or inferior to others, and above all with these changes – no more placing any of life's unneeded stress on yourself. Congratulations for taking the first positive step forward.

INTRODUCTION

Creating Balance in your life bestows
Contentment, Peace and Love in all areas of your existence

Creating balance was a lesson you probably learned early in life. Back then you couldn't comprehend what an impact this would become in your life. Remember the teeter-totter that was one of your favorite playground rides? Once you played on it for a while, you figured out that you needed the same weight on both sides to leave your feet dangling in the breeze. Everything in life needs balance.

We all experience stress in our busy lifestyles but it is how we react to this stress that is the difference between being a balanced individual or merely surviving life. We need to be able to switch gears between responsibilities among work duties, home duties, spouses, family, friends and other important functions within our lives with a smooth transition. One area can't be excessive without disrupting another and upsetting the apple cart.

Stress is one of the leading factors that create a disrupting atmosphere and it can carry over into every aspect of your life. If not resolved this can grow too unmanageable proportions and it will seem as if life is spiraling out of control. Stress is a repetitive disorder. It is many times difficult to untangle a web of stress or break its pattern to reestablish balance once again. But when you are searching for positive results you must beware of the pitfalls that lie ahead. There are six key habits to avoid when you are trying to reduce stress and optimize your health. These will be discussed further in this book as you discover the most beneficial ways to remain healthy and stress-free.

Placing balance and control back in your life starts with one important ingredient, this ingredient is *you*. Do you have negative thoughts or make negative comments. Acting on negative impulses can only result in negative responses. Sometimes we damage our reputation, lose the respect of others, push friends away, and suffer defeat at the hands of negative thoughts. Discovering your strengths, as well as your fears and weaknesses will help you become aware of why you sometimes hold a negative perspective on life. Changing your perspective to thinking positive, defeating the stress that imprisons you, and learning relaxation skills that can facilitate mental and physical health can stabilize your well-being. 'Me' time is part of our balancing strategy - this is the time to stop and relax, reflect, plan, and regain perspective over our day-to-day routines. To some this may come effortlessly, to others such as perfectionists or overachievers this may be a struggle to be learned. These changes will permanently enhance your life, your health, and your interactions with others.

Skills that you will learn to Create Balance in your life?

Mind skills	*Body skills*
Identify your fears	Nourishment
Defeat stress	Health
Develop positive thinking	Relieve Tension
Relaxation techniques	Physical Fitness

To defeat stress and conquer life you will need to be flexible yet self disciplined to gain control over your mind and body. The skills you develop while learning to triumph over stress and your ability to eradicate fear and negativity from your life will be your most valuable asset for the remainder of your days.

When you learn how to identify your negative behaviors and take the necessary steps to correct these self-limiting actions, you will experience remarkable changes in your life. Boundaries will be limitless, your mind will be at peace and in harmony with your body, you will achieve things you have only dreamed of, and find greater happiness and inner peace. You will then maintain control in your life by applying a magnitude of relaxation techniques along with physical and mental balance as you unearth the mind and body connection.

At this level of advancement you will have the ability to spread your knowledge to help others create balance in there lives. There is no better gift to offer than to celebrate life as it was meant to be celebrated.

Enjoy each day that passes for none of them can ever be replaced or relived.

Happiness Always, Susan

Stress is one of the primary causes of negative thinking. We have the ability to make our life more satisfying and more fulfilling, by learning to live more in balance with our environment. We can eliminate the feelings of being stressed, overwrought, uptight, and anxious and replace these with stress-free, peaceful, calm, and tranquil. I wanted to master this and I know you do also. So let's get started on our journey of soul searching and removing the negative from your life and replace this with the positive.

Everyone experiences stress in their lives. When stress accumulates or becomes chronic it begins to take its toll on both your mental, as well as your physical health. Sometimes, you are placed in a stressful environment that can be manipulated to reduce the effects of stress, such as a work environment. Other stressors may have been brought forward from your past experiences and inadvertently placed in your present day circumstances. Any type of stress that disrupts your life is a stress that needs to be addressed and eliminated.

Traumatic experiences, verbal or physical abuse, mental stress, and psychological disorders such as bipolar disease, phobias, or obsessive compulsive disorder are examples of events and mental disturbances that intensify stress levels. The consequences of these major life alterations are a build up of insecurities and negative impressions that have left an imprint in the mind of the victim. These consequences then multiply as the fears, past experiences, and imagination that create a negative perception in many other areas of your life. Self esteem is low, cultivating trust in another individual is difficult, and a feeling of helplessness causes uncertainty when having to make decisions.

Your overall perception of life becomes a place where doom is always just round the corner. Anxiety is high and daily stressors, or life changes generate tension in your mind and body that seem to be unbearable at times. To conquer these negative reactions we must first understand how and why they control us.

Let's catch a glimpse into Morgan's life as she perceives it.

Morgan stood in front of the sliding glass doors. There was a glimpse of something there, something on the other side. She placed the palm of her hand and fingertips on the glass. It was cold to the touch. There seemed to be a slight movement on the other side of the glass. As she looked closer, looked through the pane she caught a glimpse of a familiar face, the reflection of herself, a fragmented piece of her life that she no longer could connect with but was only a haunting memory of her past. She looked at the hand pressed against the glass on the other side. She wanted so desperately to reach through the pane and reunite with her other self. She felt so alone. The tears trickled down her cheeks but in her eyes there wasn't a reflection of pain it was a reflection of sadness, a stare into nowhere, her thoughts moving her through a maze. She was helplessly searching for a way out, a way to the other side.

This is one of the ways that Morgan views depression. Being one person separated by some force, each feeling and living in a different dimension. They move parallel with each other never able to reach out and connect as one, both moving as if being programmed and directed by an unseen entity. Every moment being weighted and heavy, every second stretching as if put into slow motion. Doing what needed to be done but not understanding why, accept that she had an obligation to continue the battle.

She tells me as I listen intently holding the phone piece that was fixed to my ear. Listening to her words of despair and feeling her heartbreak as she describes her loss. "I know there is another world beyond this window, one where people feel joy in their heart and look forward to what tomorrows will unfold and although I want to be part of that I somehow feel comfortable where I am. I'm alone but there is no confusion, it's safer, it's quiet."

Morgan is one of the lost souls frozen by fear. Anxiety disorders, depression, bipolar disease, and/or phobias can compound each other and cause devastating results. Results that steal lives and separate families. Still, once these conditions are brought under control with the help of physicians and therapists, there are additional issues to be resolved. There will be built up fears to be banished, self esteem to be built, and balance to be reestablished in Morgan's life to untangle the thoughts and fears that created these multiple results. We'll check back in with Morgan a little later.

Even in an altered state our minds are powerful. We can fall prey to our minds imagination. This invisible entity takes a firm hold on our thoughts and emotions. The feelings become real yet you can vaguely sense a shadow of illusion, like Morgan viewing the shadow on the other side of the glass. Mental illnesses are widespread, some seek help and others stumble through their lives hoping tomorrow will hold the answers that finally give them peace and happiness.

Are you suffering from any abnormal thought patterns? Let's take a look at some forms of stress to see if you may be able to identify with any of these underlying symptoms or anxiety disorders.

Stress is a feeling experienced when a person perceives that the demands placed on them, surpasses their capability to reach a successful outcome. Loss of control in any situation can project the feelings of fear and this will escalate to stress. It is your perceptions and expectations that will determine the level, if any, of stress that you will experience. Stress in any form can produce negative behavior and thought patterns.

One of the most well known types of stress is ***acute stress***. This type of stress activates what has been termed your "flight-or-fight response." This is your body's reaction to a threat, challenge, or scare. It is a reflex that signals to your body that you may be entering a threatening situation. Your body then automatically changes its chemistry to prepare to defend itself or flee from danger. The acute stress response is immediate, it's intense, and in certain circumstances, it can be thrilling as your body experiences an immediate rush of adrenalin when you become frightened, such as jumping out of a plane on your first skydiving experience.

Your body's reaction to stress will cause increased blood pressure and heart rate, sweaty palms, shaking, nausea, and shortness of breath. The hormone that releases adrenaline will boost the supply of oxygen and glucose to the brain and muscles, this prepares the body to defend itself, at the same time the release of adrenaline will suppress other non-emergency bodily processes for instance the digestion system. At the same time a breakdown of lipids in fat cells is occurring, which will release stored energy.

Almost everyone has experienced these changes in the body. For instance, you are driving along and another vehicle all of a sudden hits his breaks in front of you. You have to react fast. This causes a jolt of energy due to the sudden increase of instantaneous fear. When this happens, your body signals your hormones for help. You clutch the steering wheel with a tight grip and at the same time your foot slams on the brakes as you come to a screeching halt. Your heart is beating fast, your breathing has increased, your hands are shaking, and an overwhelming feeling of fear surrounds your being. After you acknowledge that the immediate threat has passed and you are safe, your body should begin to self-regulate. This will begin to decrease the hormone levels triggering your body's response, and return them to their normal functioning.

The negative response that may appear in this example might be displaced anger. You may jump to the conclusion that it was the person driving the vehicle in front of you that almost caused you to become involved in an accident. But what if it wasn't that persons fault but the one ahead of him or possibly an animal ran out in front of him or he's having a heart attack. Okay I may have stretched it a little with the heart attack. The point is that you are immediately looking at the negative in the situation. The positive may not have even entered your mind. You didn't have an accident, nobody got hurt, your car didn't receive any damage, you may even have taken part in saving an animals life. To top it off you may not even have entertained the thought that this person didn't intentionally stop dead in his tracks so that you would become angered and fearful and possibly injured. Have you ever unintentionally made an error in your driving skills that affected another individual?

Since we can't prepare for or expect the unexpected, there is no way to avoid this type of stress, only our reaction to it. Your body's reaction to stress is a natural reaction to self preservation and is a beneficial type of stress. This stress requires no treatment or medications to alleviate its effects.

Chronic stress results from long-term exposure to acute stress. This response is much more subtle in its activation than the acute stress response, but the effects are more problematic due to the duration of the symptoms. This category of stress is one that you feel when you are continuously in an environment that causes you undue stress. Under these circumstances, the very stress response intended to protect you from harm can do you harm. Sometimes your stress hormone system fails to shut off and goes into overdrive.

The difference between your feelings of acute stress and chronic stress is the length of time that your body is subjected to these altered states. While acute stress may ignite increased blood pressure and heart rate, sweaty palms, shaking, nausea, shortness of breath, and other possible symptoms, it is the chronic stress that has more dangerous effects since these feelings are prolonged rather than short and sporadic. (Susan Perry, 2006, 24) "Chronic stress has been linked to a host of physical complaints, including headaches, fatigue, back and neck problems, irritable bowel syndrome, heartburn, diarrhea and skin problems. It can weaken your immune system, leaving you more susceptible to colds, the flu and other infections. And most disturbing of all, it can lead to heart attacks and stroke. The constant bombardment of chronic stress takes its toll on your body. If you ignore stress it won't go away. If you allow stress to continue it may literally kill you."

There are life changing events that cause higher degrees of stress than day to day living. Examples of some of these experiences are listed below.

Death of a loved one	Changing schools
Birth of a child	Beginning a new school year
Start of a new relationship	Arrested and/or placed in jail

Children leaving home	Financial issues
Divorce or breakup of a relationship	Sexual difficulties
Health issues	Holidays
Marriage	Violence in school
Retirement	Peer pressures
Loss of a job	Work overload
Personality conflicts	

The instances above involve not only very strong emotions but a mix of many different emotions. These types of stress are usually referred to as a crises or a life change. In addition to causing a high degree of stress, in some circumstances, this may graduate to an advanced disorder such as generalized anxiety disorder or post traumatic disorder. This is due to the type of event that is experienced, how it is perceived by the individual, and how it is specifically dealt with in the terms of mental health. (More on anxiety disorders in Chapter 2).

Let's use for example, the death of a loved one to reveal the mix of emotions that can take place in the mind. When someone experiences a death whether it is expected or sudden, the emotions are similar. Stages of development may include denial, anger, depression and then acceptance. Not every individual will go through each stage or they will go through each stage in varying degrees.

There are ways that you can help the individual pass through the stages of development that will ultimately lead them to acceptance. If you are the one who has lost someone very dear to you, then being aware of the stages will let you understand the normalcy of each stage. This will also give you ways to define your grief and help you to adapt and re-enter the world. The most important thing you can do to help someone is to let the person talk it out. Be there as their sounding board and if needed, suggest speaking to a grief counselor.

Even though death is apparent, it becomes a difficult reality when you have spent time and developed an attachment to the one who has been lost. The survivors are the ones who are left behind suffering and battling confusing emotions. Due to the shock of the loss of a loved one the individual may function through days in a dreamlike state of mind just moving from one moment to the next. Our feelings of denial and disbelief—"I was just talking to him yesterday" or "I can't believe this is happening"—may suggest guilt as we are plagued with the question of "why," which we can't answer.

Death is something that is out of our control therefore we tend to lash out with frustration and deal with feelings of helplessness and possible outbursts of anger. You blame the doctors for the death—"Why couldn't they have done better?" You blame yourself, "I should have been able to do more." You may even blame God, "How could you let this happen?" Your anger can be projected onto others as well as projected directly at the person who you feel has abandoned you and left you behind.

As days pass you might entertain several thoughts about how others should perceive death. As they try to cheer you up and lighten your load you wonder how they can seem so carefree, how they can smile at a time like this when there is so much grief and heartache. You feel that they should be experiencing the pain that you are feeling. The anger stage can intensify these negative thoughts. You know that your friends and family are there to help you. The ability to reach out and express your emotions to another is advantageous to your recovery.

Dwelling on negative emotions can further lead to depression. It becomes important to acknowledge your feelings and find the answers to your negative thoughts. You may not have had the time to say your good-byes to someone who has past suddenly, or you may feel abandoned, alone, and defeated by the circumstances that have been dealt to you. You understand and can differentiate between unintended death and an intentional abandonment in pursuit of something different. You understand that truly nobody is alone unless it is of their choice. You have the logical answers to all of the questions inside of you no matter what they are and once you reach acceptance you will have answered all of your questions.

Take baby steps to gradually re-enter the world. As time goes on small depressions will be normal as you see or hear things that bring back special memories that you had shared with this individual. Some will tend to blind themselves from the loved ones faults and place them on a pedestal of perfection. If this is a spouse this may implant the idea that nobody could ever be able to take their place and therefore they stop looking for happiness. It is important to appreciate that all persons are unique and in that essence they can never be replaced, yet happiness is not forever out of reach. Thoughts will need to be altered to release any guilt and realize that moving on is not betraying their love or memories as these will always remain close at heart. Thresholds of pain, anger and fear are not the same for everyone. There is no set timeframe to follow, to accept death, to move on, or to start another relationship. Our universe as well as our being is based on balance, which includes the giving of life and the taking of life. You must believe and accept as fact that their spirit and soul lives on.

When you are temporarily overcome by a crisis that immerses you into a negative thinking pattern with bouts of anxiety there are many natural stress reduction techniques that can help you to progress through these times of difficulties. Our objective is to place focused thought into a project that allows our minds to relax and break away from the negative impact. Possibilities include such ideas as becoming submersed in a hobby such as drawing, painting or gardening. Other positive alternatives would be guided imagery meditation or writing therapy. (See Chapter 8 for more relaxation techniques.)

All individuals experience life changes as they grow and advance through life. These may be prompted by a major change such as moving to a new area, taking on a new job, or getting a promotion. When changes such as this occur, it will take several months to adjustment and accept these new beginnings. This period in time is a crucial turning point in your life that alters your direction and sends you to follow a different path. This advances our life from one that held familiar qualities of which we were comfortable with, to the unfamiliar side of life which generates feelings of discomfort.

Changes encourage us, or sometimes push us, to step out of our comfort zone. When this occurs the high amounts of stress that are experienced are due to fear of the unknown as well as the vast number of changes that we are experiencing simultaneously. There are still many advantages and positive effects to take into consideration through these changes. Keep your focus pulled to recognize the positive in your situation, when a negative thought enters, replace it with positive fact. Changing and growing opens many new doors of discovery.

Any stress, whether acute or chronic, or whether caused by crises, or life change, can affect our health in many negative ways. As stated by Dr. William J, Knaus (1994) in his writings on Change your life now; he categorizes destructive stress as d-Stress and contends that, "Stress can be uncomfortable when you feel tied up in knots. It becomes destructive when that feeling lingers and you experience a stress overload. Depending on your make-up, this destructive stress can cause high cholesterol, heart disease, depression, ulcers, attention and concentration deficiencies, memory loss, neurogenia (chronic fatigue), and other unpleasant symptoms."

When these reactions to stress occur in your body they can cause minor physical or emotional symptoms, which can be an alert of stress overload. The following list contains both physical and mental symptoms of stress, along with some behavioral traits, that may indicate that an abundance of stress is present in your life.

It is crucial that you consult with your health care provider and share your list of symptoms to ensure you are not suffering from a more serious condition.

Physical and Mental Symptoms
This list in part was obtained from MayoClinic.com

√ acne
√ anemia
√ anger
√ anxiety
√ avoids risks
√ become controlling
√ chest pain
√ concern of losing control
√ confusion
√ constipation
√ continuous mood shifts
√ decreased productivity
√ depression
√ diarrhea
√ dizziness
√ extreme distress
√ fatigue
√ feel insecure
√ feelings of hopelessness
√ feelings of inadequacy
√ forgetfulness
√ frustration
√ guilt
√ have irrational thoughts
√ headaches
√ helplessness

√ isolation of self
√ jaw clenching
√ jealousy
√ job burnout
√ judgmental, critical
√ lack drive
√ lack interest in any hobbies
√ lack of compassion
√ loss in sexual drive
√ low aspirations
√ low self esteem
√ lowered immunity
√ nail biting
√ nausea
√ over react to events
√ panic attacks
√ poor time management
√ pounding heart
√ procrastination
√ rash – hives
√ shaking
√ shortness of breath
√ stomach cramping
√ substance abuse
√ suicidal thoughts
√ swallowing difficulty

√ high blood pressure

√ high cholesterol

√ impatience

√ increased perspiration

√ indigestion

√ insomnia

√ teeth grinding

√ ulcers

√ unable to concentrate

√ unmotivated

√ worry

Behavioral Traits

√ apprehension of criticism or disapproval of others

√ bothered about physical appearance

√ mind racing/chatter

√ eating disorders – anorexia or bulimia

√ entertain thoughts and fear of dying

√ frowning, wrinkled forehead, worry lines, and wrinkles

√ have no response to challenge

√ phobia of social embarrassment

√ physical tension - neck pain or back pain

√ sickly - colds, flu, upset stomach, or heartburn

√ tendency to shun responsibility

Your body's reaction to the symptoms of stress may include more serious and potentially devastating consequences related to the heart. When your body increases the blood clotting in your system you may develop ongoing problems with high blood pressure. This will increase your risk of heart attack. Also, if prolonged an increase in your cholesterol and triglycerides levels can result in heart disease or stroke.

Dr. William J, Knaus (1994) "D-stress can affect our bodies in many ways, from gastrointestinal distress to cardiovascular dysfunction. D-stress tops the list of serious health problems of our times." Most individuals take having a healthy heart for granted. This blinding problem is due to lack of information focused on the devastating effects of stress on the body. Stress is one of the leading factors in heart disease.

Additional effects of stress on the body, namely tension, can advance to physical pain, headaches and sleep disorders. These may be the start of layering or compounding one issue or symptom upon another without resolve. There is a huge impact that stress plays in our every day life and added variables such as pain can intensify the effects of stress on both the body and mind.

The human body can be a contradictory subject. It is an incredible and complicated structure. It is strong yet fragile, durable yet delicate, muscular yet flexible. Pain associated with our body can be subtle but yet sometimes very obvious. These warnings of pain are a means of self preservation and protection against further structural damage.

Painful episodes such as headaches caused by stress, can affect many areas of your life by restricting the performance of normal activities. When pain and stress run concurrent with each other our emotions are heightened as we are faced with feelings of frustration, fatigue and aggravation. This mixture of variables can lead to emotional outbursts. Hence, the results of even more stress are introduced.

Common forms of headaches are termed - tension, cluster, and migraine. These can be caused by a psychological overload caused by stress, depression, head injury, eye strain, low blood sugar, anxiety, and sinusitis among others. Headache pain is one of our built in alarms that signals the mind that the body is experiencing distress. Migraine is a neurological disorder that generally involves repeated headaches. Some people also have nausea, vomiting, and other symptoms. Most people suffering from migraine headaches do not have any warning before it occurs.

(Susan Perry, 2006, 148) "Migraine Headache: Dull throbbing pain, often on one side of the head, accompanied by nausea. Before the headache occurs, you may experience vision disturbances, such as flickering lights. A migraine headache can last from 4 to 72 hours."

Visual disturbances are called an aura before the headache starts. These headaches are often classified based on whether they include this early symptom. Most of these headaches do not have this aura stage. This type of head pain is caused by abnormal brain activity, which is triggered by such things as stress or food. It seems to involve various nerve pathways and chemicals in the brain. The changes affect blood flow in the brain and surrounding membranes.

When this disorder begins with visual disturbances (aura), these warning symptoms may occur anywhere from a few minutes to 24 hours before the headache. The visual changes are common in one or both eyes and may occur in any combination:

Seeing flashing lights	Sensitivity to bright light
Other visual hallucinations	Blurred vision
Temporary blind spots	Eye pain

Onset of this disorder without the aura stage may include:

Throbbing, pulsating headache	Feeling that the room is moving (vertigo)
Usually worse on the sides of the forehead	Loss of appetite
May be on only one side of the forehead	Nausea
May be severe or dull	Vomiting
Commonly lasts 4 to 72 hours	Fatigue

To remove negative stressors from your life such as pain you must deal with the pain. If there are options you have that will reduce pain then all of these options should be examined. Some controls that you may find helpful to use to overcome pain may be:

Professional help – Seek the help of a professional medical doctor, pain clinic, or a chiropractic physician to reduce the pain.

Music - Listening to soothing music and using stress breathing techniques are an anytime, anywhere escape from the daily stressors that you face.

Acupuncture - Nerves, muscles and connective tissue of the body are stimulated by way of needles releasing endorphins and increasing blood flow.

Delegate – Cut down your to-do list. Only do what is absolutely necessary and delegate any tasks possible to both reduce your activity and/or repetitive actions and focus on the most important matters.

Walking –A simple stress free walk can help strengthen your muscles as well as quiet the mind and relax the body.

Stress Management – Place additional focus on stress management techniques to maintain a healthy balance and control over all areas of your life.

Meditation – 30 minutes a day or short 10 minute intervals at work to meditate or relax in a quiet, dim setting can rejuvenate your body, clear your mind, and reduce tension.

Spa Massage – This is used for a multiple of reasons, pain and stress relief are two common reasons for many individuals to seek treatment. Theories behind what massage might do include blocking pain signals to the brain, stimulating the release of endorphins and serotonin, improving sleep, decreasing muscle tension, increasing flexibility and blood flow, which all make the body relaxed and better able to function.

When any of the symptoms or negative thought patterns discussed throughout this first chapter, are left unattended, they can cause turmoil and disruption in many areas of an individual's life. This can also lead to bouts with depression as a result of not gaining control in these areas and disrupting the life balance that helps to diffuse the negativity and produce the inner calmness.

What can be even more disturbing are the effects that anti-depressants can have within the body and how they can affect the mind. Anti-depressants are a secondary form of treatment since they do nothing to permanently resolve what the cause of the depression is. This leads to our first habit to be avoided and is explained further in depth below.

The **first** key habit to avoid when attempting to reduce stress that may cause us even more stress and cause damage to our health is the taking of anti-depressants.

Anti-depressants – When you are stressed you may turn to anti-depressants. / These can lead to unhealthy thoughts of suicide and many side effects that cause stress. / So you take more anti-depressants.

The side effects alone should be enough to convince you that this can increase your stress and effect your health, they range from; weight gain or loss, intense restlessness, insomnia, fatigue, sexual dysfunction, panic attacks, anxiety, increase in suicidal behavior, dry mouth, nausea, nervousness, headache, tiredness, dry mouth, constipation, increased heart rate, increased cholesterol levels, agitation, and may also cause increase blood pressure in some people.

Be aware that drugs may help you feel better in the short term, but they cannot offer you a cure. If the anti-depressant is prescribed on a temporary basis by your family physician they will most likely not refer you to a counselor to decipher the root of the problem. If you feel this is an issue that will not disappear with time you must be responsible to seek help yourself, or ask for a referral to a stress management counselor, life coach, or psychologist, otherwise, once the medication runs out the problem may resurface. Keep in mind that if you should feel like you no longer need the medication, it is advisable to consult your physician so that you can slowly be weaned off of the medicine to avoid any of the withdrawal symptoms.

There has been a rapid growth in the interest of stress management and stress counseling. These counselors, if you choose to visit one can help you identify the underlying causes of your stress. They can help you understand how it affects you both physically and emotionally. They can also help you recognize the warning signs so that you are prepared to counteract the next attack should it occur.

Depressions as with Morgan, can take on many different faces. Morgan felt confined, trapped, isolated from the outside world, and stuck in the fear that her mind was dictating. Although Morgan missed the interaction with the world on the other side of the pane, she was also growing to accept her captivity and she began to embrace the escape from the outside world she had grown to know.

If you feel you are suffering from depression, look for symptoms and negative thinking patterns such as:

Sadness – A feeling of weakness or loss. These individuals tend to withdrawal from society, friends and family. They may retreat when there are people present or become quiet.

Anxiety – Anxiety will usually generate feelings of fear, apprehension, or worry. This may cause noticeable physical sensations such as heart palpitations, nausea, and chest pain, shortness of breath, stomach aches or headaches.

Social anxiety – This is anxiety symptoms that appear each time that you are put in a situation where groups of people are around you. Sometimes even the thought of this, such as a meeting that you must attend, will bring about the symptoms of social anxiety before you actually enter into this environment.

Guilt – Feelings of guilt can be generated in two different ways – one being that the individual has the feeling that they have done something that they shouldn't have done or two, the individual feels that they should be doing something that they are not.

Sleep Patterns – Depression may cause a sleep pattern to fluctuate to extremes. The individual may sleep continuously or have bouts of insomnia caused by such things as worry, fear, or continuous mind chatter.

Loneliness – As with Morgan, the individual may feel a sense of emptiness with depression. Even when in voluntary withdrawal they may feel disconnected and alienated from other people.

Confusion - The individual may experience thoughts that overlap other thoughts. This can cause a sense of whirling confusion with the inability to focus on one issue at a time.

Changes in Appetite – Appetite is a symptom of depression that can fluctuate in either direction. Some individuals in a depressive state will eat in an attempt to make themselves feel better or feel happy again, while others will not have any desire to take part in the ritual of eating.

Fatigue – Physical fatigue as well as mental fatigue can play a part when experiencing depression. There may be no desire to get up from bed due to the feeling of being worn-out, exhausted, or weary. Mental fatigue may show itself by feelings of being drained, drowsy, or have a lack of concentration.

Depersonalization – In an attempt to deaden or numb emotions this may trigger an individual to use recreational drugs to try to overcome the negative feelings they are experiencing. The use of drugs or alcohol may give them a temporary diversion from life as if they are living in another's body or in a dreamlike state of mind.

Chronic pain – Sometimes there are episodes of pain that cannot be explained. It is important to note that pain is subjective in nature and is defined by the individual experiencing the pain. The medical community's understanding of chronic pain now includes the impact that the mind has in processing and interpreting pain signals.

Suicidal feelings – The individual who is overwhelmed with feelings of sadness may have thoughts of ending their life and make plans or attempts to commit suicide.

Solitude – Individuals may pull away from all interaction with other persons. They want to be left by themselves without interruption. One reason may be because they feel they can not deal with any other issues, even the pressure to entertain or strike up conversations may seem like a tedious task.

Anger – Anger sometimes flares up for a reason that would not have typically affected that person. There may be times that the individual cannot distinguish why the anger was ignited except that they had feelings of frustration and irritability. These feelings may cause an outburst that lashes out at the closest person to them. They may be viewed as being rude or ill-mannered.

When experiencing symptoms of depression it is essential to look for the root of the problem. Once this is discovered you may find many other ways to relieve the depression other that anti depressants. Utilize relaxation techniques and pull your minds focus from the outside world to the inside peace to work on problem solving skills that will put you back in control.

Many of these symptoms and negative thought patterns of depression, such as anger, will cause major disruptions in every area of an individual's life. Anger can develop as a means of outlet for your frustrations. This can erupt at any time, which may jeopardize your job or hurt people you love without having the intentions of doing so. Anger is an uncontrollable and unpredictable behavior and therefore, can be misdirected towards individuals that are not involved with the situation that triggered the emotion. There may be flair ups when you have seen nothing that has happened visually to trigger the emotion. Irritability and moodiness are examples of this emotion which are related more to character traits than to instincts.

(The Health Care Center) "Trying to decide whether anger causes stress, or whether stress is the effect of anger, is like pondering the age-old chicken and egg dilemma. A more important question to ask yourself is which one you have more control over. We may not always be able to identify all the stressors in our lives, but we can certainly learn to control our reactions to them. Furthermore, if we can learn to control our anger, we will most likely end up feeling more in control and less stressed. Anger and stress seem to exist together, so getting rid of one of them will naturally phase out the other."

Anger is also a part of the fight/flight brain response to a perceived threat of pain. When a person makes the cognitive choice to take action to immediately stop the threatening/painful behavior of another, anger becomes the predominant feeling. Pain or the threat of pain can be perceived from written threats to verbal insults. We may not perceive an immediate physical threat, but pain can be felt psychologically making the threat of psychological harm real. This emotion can arise without a direct physical threat or an actual other person present, such as a letter being tacked up on your door by a knife. Because of our capacity to image the distant future, the threat of pain can also arise purely from our imagination, and not be based on anything happening in the immediate present.

For better understanding of the anger/fear connection, think of a time when you felt threatened. Perhaps you were driving along when another car suddenly pulled out in front of you. There was a very quick onset of fear that caused you to leap into action, but when the fear subsided didn't you feel anger towards that person that pulled out in front of you? "Why did you feel irritated?" You know the person didn't intentionally pull into your path – that's why these events are called accidents. Yet, they made you fearful of the threat of harm and that turned into anger. It is at times like these that an individual who already suffers from a control problem with anger may flare up into an extreme rage, their temper becomes uncontrollable and the outcome may involve violence.

If you, a friend or a family member suffer from fits of intense anger it's time to acknowledge this problem and seek help to gain control over this part of your life. Negative thinking patterns that result in anger can be dangerous and destructive. If you think that by not being physical or revealing your outbursts that this will help or resolve the issue you need to stop and think again. The negative thoughts generated in your mind still affect the body even if there isn't any outward burst of rage. Sometimes depression may be caused by rage and frustration turned inwards.

For Morgan both inward rage and outward rage reared their evil heads. Although Morgan seemed calm on the exterior, her insides contradicted this with reactions of outbursts that caused an eruption of anger to explode without control. At these times it would always cause a rage that was only satisfied with the release of destructive actions. The nearest object became the victim and the harder it was thrown the more emotional relief was experienced. Then, as quick as the anger erupted it subsided leaving the shattered evidence as its only witness. Morgan was not responsible for her actions as she had no clue of what was happening or what was causing these behaviors. What's more is she didn't know why they started, or how to change them.

Management of these emotions commonly refers to Anger management techniques: this is a system of psychological therapeutic techniques and exercises by which, someone with excessive or uncontrollable behavior can control or reduce the triggers, degrees, and effects of this emotional state.

There are two forms of negative behavior associated with anger and these are categorized as Passive anger or Aggressive anger.

To detect passive anger look for symptoms of:

Secretive behavior - stockpiling resentments that are expressed behind people's backs, giving the silent treatment or under the breath mutterings, avoiding eye contact, putting people down, gossiping, anonymous complaints, poison pen letters, stealing, and conning.

Ineffectualness – can cause deviant behavior including setting yourself and others up for failure, choosing unreliable people to depend on, being accident prone, underachieving, sexual impotence, expressing frustration at insignificant things but ignoring serious ones.

Manipulation - provoking people to aggression and then patronizing them, forgiveness, provoking aggression but staying on the sidelines, emotional blackmail, false tearfulness, feigning illness, sabotaging relationships, using sexual provocation, using a third party to convey negative feelings, withholding money or resources.

Dispassion - giving the cold shoulder or phony smiles, dampening feelings with substance abuse, overeating or oversleeping. This person may not respond to another's anger, be frigidity, give excessive amounts of time to machines, objects or intellectual pursuits, talking of frustrations but showing no feeling.

Self-blame – this can show itself in an action such as apologizing too often, being overly critical, inviting criticism.

Evasiveness - turning your back in a crisis, avoiding conflict, not arguing back, becoming phobic.

Self-sacrifice - being overly helpful, making do with second best, quietly making long suffering signs but refusing help, or lapping up gratefulness.

Obsessive behavior - needing to be clean and tidy, making a habit of constantly checking things, over-dieting or overeating, demanding that all jobs are done perfectly.

To detect aggressive anger look for symptoms of:

Threats - frightening people by saying how you could harm them or their property, finger pointing, fist shaking, wearing clothes or symbols associated with violent behavior.

Grandiosity - showing off, expressing mistrust, being a poor loser, wanting center stage all the time, not listening, talking over people's heads, expecting kiss and make-up sessions to solve problems.

Destructiveness – may result in the destruction of objects, harming animals, destroying a relationship between two people, reckless driving, alcohol abuse.

Vengeance - refusing to forgive and forget, bringing up hurtful memories from the past.

Bullying - threatening people directly, persecuting, pushing or shoving, using power to oppress, shouting, playing on people's weaknesses.

Unpredictability - explosive rages over minor frustrations, attacking indiscriminately, dispensing unjust punishment, inflicting harm on others for the sake of it or expressing illogical arguments.

Unjust blaming - accusing other people for your own mistakes, blaming people for your own feelings, making general accusations.

Selfishness – ignoring other's needs and not responding to requests for help.

Manic – may be seen in the individual by them speaking too fast, walking too fast, working too much and expecting others to fit in, driving too fast, reckless spending.

Road Rage - behavior such as tailgating, excessively blowing a car horn, and speeding.

Hurtfulness - physical violence, verbal abuse, biased or vulgar jokes, breaking a confidence, playing loud music, using foul language or ignoring people's feelings.

All of these symptoms of anger are destructive, but let's focus a moment on road rage since this may be more of a stressor that we place on ourselves that we can easily rectify. Road rage is an act of anger and violent behavior by a driver of an automobile, which can cause accidents or incidents on roadways.

Without any visible facts, this emotion is usually labeled and ticketed as careless or reckless driving. When a scene is escalated it may result in charges of assault and battery, or if a victim is killed, vehicular homicide.

As knowledge of this offense continues to grow over time with the increased population and congested roadways more serious penalties are inevitable and well warranted. The only state that I am aware of at this point in time that penalizes for this offense in the United States is the state of California. This state has placed into law a penalty for a court-ordered suspension specifically directed towards road rage. Of course this doesn't mean that other states haven't and won't follow their lead.

What causes Road Rage?

There are a number of causes for road rage, but of course stress is the most likely number 1 leading factor. This is another stressor that people mostly place upon themselves. Individuals are trying to accomplish too many things in a short period of time. Rather than saying no, cutting some items from their to-do list, or rearranging their schedule they continue their pressurized timetable without a second thought as to the pressure they are placing upon themselves. So with this, they are in a rush to get somewhere and are usually running behind schedule. They are focused on themselves and their watch. They tailgate, speed, rubber neck, cut a driver off without signaling, and change lanes frequently as they try to get one more car length ahead. When you are waiting patiently for a parking space, this person will be the one who immediately swings out in front of you to cut you off and take the space that just opened up.

Outside influences that contribute to road rage can be a multiple of distractions such as cell phone usage, eating, drinking, yelling at the children, and primping as they drive. This can affect cars in front of them and also behind them. If they are not paying attention when all of a sudden traffic in front of them has slowed, they can end up rear ending another vehicle or breaking fast and causing the vehicle behind them to lose control.

I hate to be the bearer of bad news but there is no way that you can intentionally avoid road rage since you only have control over your reactions, which basically means although you can't avoid it, you can be one of those special people who don't contribute to it.

Things you can do to help are:

- Leave yourself plenty of time to travel taking into consideration possible traffic delays.

- Use relaxation techniques in your vehicle such as aromatherapy and listening to soothing music CD's.
- Be considerate of other drivers (yes, even if it is *Those* driver's) – Remember you only have control over how you react.
- If someone signals that they need to enter the lane ahead of you – slow down and let them in.
- Use your signals to let other drivers behind you know of your intentions to slow down and make a turn.
- Don't try to race by a couple of vehicles to get ahead when you have intentions of exiting a highway. When someone is entering a highway move over and let them in or lift off of your gas to give them time and space to enter.
- Never tailgate, keep a safe distance for unprepared breaking.
- If someone is rude to you, don't give them the satisfaction of losing your temper, ignore them and take pleasure in knowing you are not satisfying their need for acknowledgement.

Above all the rest, remember that they may truly be experiencing an emergency so give the other driver the benefit of the doubt. We are all prone to making driving error's so don't jump to the conclusion that this person intentionally singled you out of the crowd to be rude to. You never know when the driver next to you is distracted and could make an error in judgment. Defensive driving is safe driving.

When anger is an issue that has become unmanageable then anger management skills can be learned to help bring this emotion in check. Typical anger management techniques are the use of deep breathing and meditation as a means of relaxation. (see relaxation techniques) Other interventions lean towards behavior modifications such as altering your perception, learning forgiveness, changing how you speak about yourself or others, and improving optimism.

Most important is that you have to want to change your behavior and outbursts. You were not born with anger so modifications on your thinking process will be required to control these outbursts. The difference in success or failure is not necessarily how you look, dress, or the level of education, as much as it is how you think.

In many ways we're all alike; however, one little difference can make a big difference. The little difference is attitude. You need to stop and think, what are the hidden costs and negative possibilities that can come out of an outburst of anger? Is this eruption worth it? If not, remove yourself from the immediate trigger causing this response to regain control over your emotions. Take a minute to clear and adjust your thinking process.

Other methods of anger management include:

Self Hypnosis - We all need the positive self talk that hypnosis can deliver when we are feeling low, whether it's to motivate ourselves, gain confidence in ourselves, overcome some fears or negative emotions, ease pain, or just to learn something new— another way of looking at a situation— a way to overcome a negative behavior or thought. (More on Self-Hypnosis later)

Evaluate the situation - Can you find a middle ground for agreement with another person rather than initiate a conflict.

Determine your triggers – What people, places, or things cause you to become angry. Each experience you have, note the trigger. This will help you to understand why you react negatively. Are there any changes that can be made to avoid these triggers?

Be alert – Identify the symptoms you are having when you start to sense uneasy feelings of anger. Think of what truly is making you feel this way and then direct your efforts to correcting this issue.

Review your actions and reactions – Take the time to understand what triggered your anger and why. Are you viewing things one sided and focused on self gratification or satisfaction rather than viewing the big picture?

Learn to be direct – Sometimes it is hard to come face to face with someone and speak your feelings. But short term discomfort will bring long term gain. Don't beat around the bush but take the time to calm down so that you can be effective in resolving the issue. If something upsets you at work, handle it at work. Address your questions and comments directly to the source of the indifference. Indicate your feelings clearly and honestly.

Stay focused – When you are discussing your feelings stick to the facts that are causing the emotion to surface don't bring up irrelevant or past material just because you are emotional.

Be persistent to reach resolve – If you have to end the conversation before resolve has been met, schedule another time within the next 24 hours that you can pick up your discussion. Not reaching resolve will only continue to allow the problem to fester.

Be open minded – View the other side of all issues to create a balance of what might be acceptable and unacceptable. This may simply be a misunderstanding.

Listen - to what is being said to you. Anger can block your ability to listen as you are focused exclusively on what has provoked these feelings.

Learning anger management techniques takes a strong desire to change. You must be willing to ask for and accept help from the people closest to you. Stress, pain, headaches, depression, and anger are all clues that lead you to suspect that there may be a more complex problem that needs to be addressed. Although, sometimes the individual themselves is blind to what others view as obvious.

We have looked at some basics of stress and what havoc it can cause in your life. We have also looked at some symptoms that may help you identify if there are issues occurring in your life that are the cause of negative thinking patterns. From this we can begin to establish if there is a higher than normal amount of stress in your life and how these stressors may affect behavior.

If you think about the symptoms of stress and the reactions that occur, you can easily observe a cycling reaction for many of these symptoms as well, for example; you will notice that stress causes anxiety, anxiety causes stress, stress causes anxiety. Stress causes illness, illness causes stress, stress causes illness. Stress causes fear, fear causes stress, stress causes fear. Stress causes depression, depression causes stress, stress causes depression etc.

As mentioned earlier, stress is a repetitive disorder and sometimes in an attempt to reduce the unrelenting cycles, we unknowingly choose harmful ways that can damage our health and contribute to even further stress. Below there are six key habits identified to avoid in order to reduce stress and optimize your health, the first of which we have already discussed.

1. **Anti-depressants** – When you are stressed you may turn to anti-depressants. / These can lead to unhealthy thoughts of suicide and many side effects that cause stress. / So you take more anti-depressants. (See page 14)

2. **Eating** - The stress of being overweight causes you to eat. / When you eat you get stressed about being overweight. / So you eat more. (See page 68)

3. **Alcohol** – Being stressed causes you to drink. / Drinking causes stress. / So you drink more. (See page 73)

4. **Sleeping Pills** – Stress causes sleep disorders. / You take sleeping pills which can cause side effects that produce stress which can cause sleep disorders. / So you take more sleeping pills. (See page 77)

5. **Money/Shopping**– When you are stressed you may spend money to make you feel good / Spending money puts you in debt escalating your stress. / So you spend more money. (See page 89)

6. **Caffeine & Nicotine** – When you are stressed at work you take a break for a cigarette or a relaxing cup of coffee / Caffeine & Nicotine can increase stress when you are under stress / you return to your job duties and in a short period of time are in need of another stress break. (See page 106)

These are six harmful combinations when it comes to stress and your bodies' reaction to stress. Some cycles can be broken by simple relaxation techniques; others may need temporary medication to give the necessary time needed to uncover the causes and modify the behavior. Behavior modification techniques and counseling attempt to alter the individual's perception in specific problem areas. Some stress disorders such as bipolar disorder can even require lifetime medication. Once the cycle is broken you should learn and keep relaxation techniques as a daily process to keep stress at bay.

Now let's take a look at what stressors may have been carried forward from our past experiences. Once identified you should be able to decipher if these stressors may have been developing over time as problems progressed. This will be step number two…this will help to draw us closer to defeating these stressors and creating the much needed balance that will help us achieve more inner peace and happiness.

CHAPTER 2
ANXIETY DISORDERS

Let's check back in with Morgan's memories of her past in her adolescent years.

"Well, the positive points were, I loved my mother, father, sister, and climbing trees. Christmas has always been my favorite time of the year. One Christmas my father worked long hours in his shop, which was a building separate from the house. My sister and I were told he was working on a surprise. One evening he came in the house and told us to put our coats on and come outside. We hurriedly got ready and followed dad out the door and headed to his shop, but he stopped and turned back towards my sister and I. We stopped waiting for him, as he looked down at us he said, "Turn around" as he pointed a finger back towards the house, and as I turned I had seen the most beautiful sight in the world. We had a two story house and as you stood in the front you could see the roof of the garage and then further up the outer wall was the windows to my bedroom. On the garage roof there were hundreds of lights, red, green and white ones. They outlined Santa in his sleigh and his reindeer that were extended across the roof and looked as if they were taking flight. I was only five but that picture is forever burned in my memory".

Morgan now loses the twinkle of happiness in her eyes as she continues. "My dad was a carpenter and a homebody. He was the one who built our house from the ground up and was still making improvements and adding additions to the house continuing its growth. My mother, on the other hand, liked to have parties and social interaction. Fighting between them escalated to great heights and it became a nightly battle. I cried myself to sleep on a regular basis and I could hear my mother yelling at my father saying, "See you're making her cry to sleep again." I began to withdraw from life and not long after, quit speaking to anyone other than my sister and I only did this if we were alone. Over the next three years my sister would always speak for me as she tried to protect me from further anger fits from my mother."

"The day soon came, it was spring and my mother called for my sister and me as we were playing outside. As we ran to the front door my mother was standing on the outside as my father stood on the inside. She looked to my sister and me and said with a blunt tone, "I'm leaving — do you want to come with me or stay with your father?" I looked to my sister for the answer, I knew I was following were she lead. We went with my mother, hugged my father goodbye and got into the vehicle. I watched my father still standing at the door as we drove down the driveway. My mother told me as she looked back at me through the rear view mirror, "Don't look back you will only make things harder on yourself," but I couldn't stop looking as I seen him grow smaller and smaller as we dove away."

"I don't know what made me start speaking again after years of silence but I'm sure my sister was glad I did. Life never got any better though, we moved from place to place, mother married six times, became an alcoholic as the majority of her husbands were, and still no matter what she did she wasn't happy…neither was I."

So, what may have caused anxiety issues in this scenario? Almost everyone will have negative stories about their past, what matters is how you handled these situations and how you coped with them then, as well as how you are coping with them now.

Let's view some anxiety disorders and see if you can relate to any of these emotions. If so, you may be able to trace these emotions back to find where they first originated. By identifying the negative events, you may bring to light parts of the past that you carried forward with you to the present. There are many causes of anxiety some of which we will briefly explore are:

- Bipolar Disorder
- Acute Stress Disorder
- Generalized Anxiety Disorder
- Anxiety / Panic Attacks
- Post Traumatic Stress Disorder
- Phobias
- Obsessive Compulsive Disorder
- Childhood Separation Anxiety
- Adult Separation Anxiety
- Social Anxiety Disorder

Bipolar Disorder

Bipolar disorder is a very complicated mood disorder. Maybe more so complicated because there are so many combinations of moods with each mood displaying many symptoms, some of which contain similar indicators to each other. There is no one pattern that can be identified that will yield an immediate diagnosis. These disturbances can go from one extreme to the next describing what most individuals express as a roller coaster ride on emotions.

Most people do not recognize this disorder in the beginning, they may believe that what they are feeling is comparable to what other people are experiencing and learn to adapt as they believe others also adapt. This disorder is a challenge to the medical field since there are no tests that can be administered to determine if you have bipolar disorder. The diagnosis is determined by the information presented by the patient including family histories, that may help to trigger a red flag and alert the physician to this diagnosis.

The four basic moods of Bipolar are:
Mania - Hypomania - Depression - Mixed States

Mania is characterized by some distinct variables such as, an extremely elevated mood, hyperactivity, unusual thought patterns, and racing thoughts. Individuals may feel indestructible and carry an inflated ego. This could trigger reckless behavior where they may take risks that they normally would not.

Hypomania is similar but less intense than mania, causing the individual to feel restless and full of energy. This person may always have a list of tasks to accomplish and without activity will be fidgety and may become impatient, agitated and appear nervous or troubled.

Depression is always significant but can run to extremes and consist of hallucinations in the worse case scenario. Distorted thoughts may cause confusion or paranoia, and this tends to lead to frustration and feelings of helplessness.

Mixed States will exhibit a mixture of two moods in tandem of each other. When hyperactive the individual may require much less sleep than normal. They may have trouble falling asleep or after a few hours of sleep they may wake feeling full of energy and unable to return to sleep.

This is not an all inclusive list containing symptoms of each state.

There is also a term called rapid cycling. (Mondimore, 2006, 51) "Currently rapid-cycling is diagnosed if the patient has four or more episodes (mania, hypomania, depression, or mixed state) in one year."

Some other effects that may be recognizable with bipolar disorder might be:

Impulsiveness – Since the individual is in such a euphoric state of mind coupled with hyperactivity and inflated ego this may cause impulsive reactions to occur. This sometimes shows itself by shopping sprees or spur of the moment trips.

Racing mind – When in the hyper state of bipolar the mind is overactive. The individual may find it difficult to quiet their mind long enough to relax and induce sleep. This will contribute to a lack of sleep or insomnia. The individual may have too many thoughts racing at one time that could cause confusion and/or the inability to concentrate in the waking hours.

Speech – Due to the racing mind and the abundance of thoughts the person may be much more talkative than usual. As they speak you may notice that they talk at a faster pace.

Attention span – Their attention span can be short and they could be easily distracted. This can cause the individual to have many tasks going at one time, jumping from one to the other.

This disorder may be further enhanced by stress. In the extreme cases, this disorder disrupts the ability to deal with normal daily activities and tasks seem to become very complex and confusing.

(Mondimore, 2006, 149) "Bipolar patients will often have had more than their share of setbacks and psychological traumas – both past and present. Because it is a genetic illness, persons with bipolar disorder often have had difficult, even traumatic childhoods. Perhaps a parent was afflicted with the illness, perhaps he or she could not or would not receive proper treatment, and the child may have suffered disruptions to family life, periods of poverty or homelessness, perhaps even physical or emotional abuse. Psychotherapy can be enormously beneficial in helping people face and work through their difficult pasts, let go of the anger, resentment, and fear that often comes out of these experiences, and move on with their lives."

The successful management of bipolar weighs a lot on the patient's knowledge of the disorder. It is very helpful to have the ability to recognize the start of an episode. They must be able to be informative, honest, and have the ability to work well with their physician. It is also important to have the support of the people closest to them.

Currently there is no cure for bipolar activity. Due to the complexity of this disorder it is hard without trial and error, to discover what medications will work to stabilize your symptoms. Therefore, it will be normal for your monitoring physician to attempt many combinations until the right balance for you is discovered. The stress and anxiety can be balanced, managed, and controlled by working with your physician and following their suggestions of medication, therapy, and relaxation techniques you will see later in this book.

ACUTE STRESS DISORDER

This individual has suffered from a traumatic event that caused personal feelings of defenselessness and vulnerability. These feelings may in turn cause the person to withdraw from society, or suppress thoughts of the fearful memories of the event. Examples of such an event would be a robbery where they were present and their life was endangered, rape, near death experiences, or observing a horrific event which impacted another individual.

Persons encountering a traumatic event that activates acute stress disorder experience intense fear, threat of death, or threat of great physical injury. Dependant on the persons proximity to the event, or if the person was personally involved as a victim, can determine how they react and the severity of the impact on their emotional state of mind.

Some symptoms that may contribute to acute stress disorder:

- Depression causing someone to confine themselves to their bed and sleep for long periods of time.
- Insomnia making them incapable of sleep for fear of dreams triggering unwanted memories or unrelenting thoughts that won't allow them to quiet their mind and relax.
- Withdrawal from society to protect themselves from future threatening episodes.
- Temporary amnesia causing their defenses to block the unpleasant memories of the event.
- Emotional detachment where the individual may feel as though they are functioning mechanically, performing tasks in a daze as if they may be outside their body. They may be able to view themselves moving but not experiencing any emotional attachment to anything in their environment.
- The use of alcohol or drugs to try to escape from the depression or force sleep to deal with the insomnia. This is also used to deafen or dull the memories and suppress feelings they may not want to deal with.

There are many support groups set up for additional help in these circumstances. They are used to allow the individual to share experiences and exchange coping strategies with others who have experienced, or are currently experiencing similar instances. Sometimes it is just good to be in an environment where you feel others can comprehend what you have been through and what you are going through.

GENERALIZED ANXIETY DISORDER

Anxiety is normal with relation to stress. This prepares us to be cautious and alert to possible harm, such as looking both ways before crossing a street for fear of being hit by a car. When the anxiety is magnified causing a constant state of worry this can escalate to generalized anxiety disorder, which can become debilitating.

(Giacobello, 2000,14) "Someone with GAD feels afraid and worried all of the time, even when there is nothing to be afraid of or worried about. Sufferers tend to believe that some disaster is about to happen. Even if they realize that their constant worrying is not necessary or helpful, the fear does not go away."

This disorder consists of a persistent sensation of apprehension concerning the unknown. This becomes unbearable and may lead to physical symptoms of trembling, muscular aches, abdominal upsets, dizziness, and irritability, headaches, insomnia, fatigue, heart palpitations, or difficulty with concentration. Depression may occur as the individual feels powerless to grasp some form of control over their life. They don't feel secure, they don't feel at peace, they are tormented by their own speculations. What if the ground collapses below my feet? What if the world ends tomorrow? What if, questions make you prone to exaggeration and highly irrational thinking. When the imagination is free to speculate without restriction this increases the number of confusing thoughts in your mind and piling on unneeded stress. Sometimes, our fear becomes a self-fulfilling prophecy and breeds negativity.

(Jacobson, 1976, 90) I think Jacobson said it best in his book, You Must Relax, when he stated that, "The best way I know to handle morbid states of worry is to *keep in mind the distinction between the issue and the attitude.* You must observe that at such moments your attitude is over tense. If you relax the excess tension present in various muscle groups, you attain a quietude of demeanor, and you are likely to report a lessened interest in the issue."

To have some form of gauge to determine if your anxiety is more than just normal you need to decipher how long, how intense, and how often these feelings of unknown or exaggerated fear control your life. Your symptoms may come and go over periods of days so that you are looking at having good days and having bad days. All in all, if the bad days outweigh the good days over time, it becomes a situation where you need to seek professional help. If left to fester and grow this can continue to escalate and move into anxiety disorders that are even more difficult to maintain any acceptable quality of life.

Sometimes individuals may have suffered from generalized anxiety disorder since they were young and it went un-noticed, but there are many other reasons why individuals procrastinate over seeking any professional help. They may not realize that it is a documented and recognized problem by the medical profession, or fear of being outcast as damaged goods or maybe labeled as mentally disabled, they may not know how or where to seek help, or possibly feel it is a financial burden that they can't afford when what they have been living with for so long has become tolerable as a way of life for them.

Let me assure you, there is a much better way to view the world. A world that is full of hope, happiness, excitement, wonder, and satisfied contentment. If you have any doubt that you may be a victim of generalized anxiety disorder it is not only to your benefit but to your family, friends, and acquaintances that you find out if there is any validity to your suspicions. Anxiety causes negative thinking and negative thinking is like a poison that spreads throughout your mind and into your body. There are many events that may occur in someone's life that can cause them to become accustomed to negative thoughts. Examples of this may be; death of a loved one, divorce, health issues, work burnout, etc. and if left to fester and spread, their whole view of the world becomes black and void of happiness.

ANXIETY / PANIC ATTACKS

Advanced anxiety disorders have devastating physical symptoms of anxiety attacks that arrive unforeseen to the victim. (Bourne, 2001, 226) "The causes of panic disorder involve a combination of heredity, chemical imbalances in the brain, and personal stress. Sudden losses or major life changes may trigger the onset of panic attacks. So can the use of so-called recreational drugs, especially cocaine or methamphetamine."

Panic attacks may cause the victim to suffer from heart palpitations, chest pains, nausea, or shortness of breath. Coping with anxiety that creates an intense fear of this nature can cause the individual to magnify the physical symptoms of anxiety attacks. This can lead to a false conclusion of feeling as if they are in imminent danger of death such as a heart attack or stroke. These attacks last minutes but the aftereffects can go on for an hour or more. The goal is to use relaxation breathing and other forms of relaxation techniques to either eliminate or decrease and reverse the attacks in as little time as possible. A daily regimen of practicing relaxation techniques should remain in place even though there have not been any recent attacks.

It is imperative that persons who suffer from this disorder learn the importance of relaxation breathing. When our blood vessels are narrow, less oxygen enters our cells. With practice, deep breathing will allow us to open the vessels and increase this oxygen flow. During a panic attack the use of relaxation breathing should start to counteract the attack and the body should begin its attempt to self-regulate. Since persons suffering from panic disorder never know when they are going to experience an attack, this can create ongoing depressions and possible seclusion as they fear being embarrassed in public if one of these attacks should occur. (See chapter 8 for breathing techniques)

If you have been coping with anxiety and have experienced the physical symptoms of anxiety attacks, it is important to seek medical attention to exclude the possibilities of a more serious illness. If your physician rules out physical complications, he/she may refer you to a psychiatrist for further assessment and to determine the treatment that would most suit you.

Depending on the intensity of your attacks if they persist, there are certain anti-anxiety drugs that can help as well as cognitive behavioral therapy, which has become increasingly popular. Behavioral therapy focuses on changing the way you perceive a situation so that the selected reaction is acceptable. The therapy works by aiming to show you how to recognize and challenge negative thoughts. You will learn how to stop and think of your reaction before you react.

(Bourne, 2001, 226) "Between 1 and 2 percent of the population has "pure" panic disorder, while about 5 percent, or one in every twenty people, suffer from panic attacks complicated by agoraphobia."

AGORAPHOBIA

Agoraphobia is diagnosed to be an anxiety and fear of being in open areas in a place that would be difficult to escape from in a time of urgency. There is additional anxiety and fear of being in a public place that would cause embarrassment to the individual if they should suffer from a panic attack with onlookers. The individual also displays anxiety in the opposite extreme where they fear being alone, whereas if they did have an attack, there would be nobody there to help them. It is beneficial when leaving your home to be accompanied by another until treatment options can be considered.

Overcoming anxiety while suffering from a panic attack is complex since the person has no control over what is causing this sudden attack of horror. Self help for anxiety deals largely with relaxation techniques that are easily accessible in any circumstance. (Bourne, 2001, 227) "Perhaps the most common feature of agoraphobia is anxiety about being far away from home or far from a "safe person" (usually your spouse, partner, a parent, or anyone to whom you have a primary attachment.) In more severe cases, you might be able to walk alone only a few yards from home or you might be housebound altogether."

Self hypnosis therapy (or auto suggestion), is a therapy in which a person hypnotizes themselves without the assistance of another person to serve as the hypnotist. There are many downloads and CD's that deal specifically with self help for anxiety. These self help CD's have the versatility to travel with you anywhere you go. This keeps your mind focused on overcoming anxiety and helps to avoid any attack from taking place. You can listen to this as you drive or even place the disk in a jog free CD player, which allows you to listen as you walk.

Other treatments used in relation to self help for anxiety are relaxation exercises such as breathing exercises, meditation, visualization, yoga and guided imagery. (See all of these examples under relaxation techniques)

Breathing Relaxation exercises are the simplest, quickest, most convenient, and one of the most effective ways to deal with the stress of agoraphobia that you can use any time and any place. As soon as you feel a panic attack coming on it is important to start your technique to diffuse the attack. Visualization will also be valuable to you during this time to overcome anxiety. You'll need to practice this technique so you will have a predetermined visualization that will trigger your body to relax and offset the attack.

The meditation, yoga, and guided imagery are techniques that can be used at home daily to maintain a relaxed pattern of thought. This furthermore relaxes the body from becoming tense. Sometimes just the fear of having an anxiety attack, may in itself trigger an attack.

It is critical to start treatment as early as possible for agoraphobia to avoid seclusion and depression from escalating. Therapists may suggest some behavior therapy in an attempt to modify your perception of the fearful events, counseling, or possibly a temporary use of anti anxiety medication.

When seeking help from a therapist, they will be interested in knowing the symptoms that you are having. These may be signs that you experience with extreme fear such as an upset stomach, chest pain, sweaty hands, hot flashes, flushed face, rapid heart beat, palpitations, trembling, trouble breathing or swallowing, dizziness, have a fear of dying, or any other noticeable symptoms. When experiencing the panic attack it is important to note how often they occur, the duration of time they are present, what if any known triggers may be responsible for the attacks, and how they negatively affect your life.

Post Traumatic Stress Disorder

Post traumatic stress disorder is a form of extreme anxiety. This can result from suffering a traumatic experience where you may have been in fear for your life or were caused great physical harm. This also can occur if you witnessed a horrific event that caused you to be terrified, which produced overwhelming psychological and emotional trauma.

Some examples may include events such as witnessing someone's death, experiencing a violent assault of rape, war (this used to be referred to as 'shell shock'), a serious accident, robbery, experiencing or witnessing childhood or adult physical, emotional, or sexual abuse, earthquakes, hurricanes, or other natural disasters such as the tsunami disaster. (Bradshaw, 1988 [a], 51) "A child witnessing his mother being battered is equivalent to the child being battered. A witness to violence is a victim of violence."

Post traumatic stress disorder can be so severe that individuals may seclude themselves from the rest of the world due to tremendous fear. These individuals feel that this is the only way they might protect themselves from any possible harm. They may not be able to drive a vehicle as a strong result of fear due to an accident. Facing the extremes of this disorder, they may withdrawal from all family and friends, not leave their home, answer their door, and sometimes not even answer the phone.

In excessive cases an individual may perform unusual acts such as sleeping under the bed rather than on the bed in an attempt to hide from an intruder. They may suffer from insomnia or fear of the dark so they keep the lights on. When asleep they may suffer from nightmares reliving the traumatic event, they attempt to stay alert and prepared to defend themselves against any violators. They may keep all curtains and shades closed so that they cannot be seen through windows. They may alienate their mate and be so wrapped up in their fear and plagued by memories of the event that they can't show any form of intimacy or affection.

The individual's life is turned upside down and changes dramatically; they can no longer function in the world or enjoy activities they once pursued. Frightening thoughts and memories occur as flashback images in their mind. These intense fears keep them edgy, nervous, and stressed. They tend to avoid any situations or places that remind them of the event, and may become detached from their surroundings as depression ensues. Drugs or alcohol may be used as an alternative as they desperately seek to escape from their reality.

The severity of the trauma, causes of anxiety attacks, and the symptoms that arise, will be some of the variables that help guide the physicians and therapists to determine the extent of treatment for the sufferer. Some other criteria that may be taken into consideration might be if the symptoms have lasted for more than a month, how it has negatively impacted the individuals functioning socially and occupationally, if they are using any avoidance tactics due to fear, if they are experiencing anxiety or flashbacks of the event or if they are having issues with insomnia or nightmares.

(Bourne, 2001, 233) "For you to receive a diagnosis of post-traumatic disorder, these symptoms need to have persisted for at least one month (with less than one month's duration, the appropriate diagnosis is "acute stress disorder"). In addition, the disturbance must be causing you significant distress, interfering with social, vocational, or other important areas of your life."

PHOBIAS

Fear of the dark and many other phobias are a large cause of anxiety both in children and in adults. Overcoming anxiety when face to face with your phobia may be possible through visualization techniques and additional treatments.

The cause of anxiety for a given phobia can usually be traced back to a traumatic event that caused a severe reaction of terror. This event, given a set of circumstances that relate to the fear can trigger the imagination to relive the trauma or withdraw from the stimulus that causes the memory to reoccur. Individuals can develop severe fears over practically anything. Phobias can be a disabling fear that forces a person into seclusion. This can also be associated with post traumatic stress disorder.

(Jacobson, 1976, 86) "Fears may become prolonged and excessive. Then they constitute a bourdon on the nervous system and may lead to disorders in other systems as well. There comes a stage in certain cases where it becomes difficult to say whether the fear is merely an exaggerated normal state or a somewhat pathological one. But if the individual fears that he will jump out of a window when in high buildings or that he may stab somebody if a knife lies about, we call the fear definitely pathological and label it a *phobia*."

Depending on the cause of anxiety and the intensity, the therapist will choose the best treatment or combination of treatments using visualization, cognitive behavioral therapy, and neuro-liguistic programming. Visualization is one way of attempting to overcome anxiety related to an intense fear. This is similar to guided imagery meditation. In this treatment the patient will enter a state of relaxation and then be asked to visualize a triggering event under supervised observation. The patient using the therapist as a crutch of safety through many sessions, continue to face their phobia in a controlled environment. Through stages the patient will become desensitized to the stimulus that is the cause of anxiety. This means that they will be introduced to the fear in minimal amounts so that they can eventually accept their fears as unsubstantiated.

With the example of fear of the dark the patient may be asked to relax and once they have entered this relaxation state, be asked to visualize a specific event that makes them uncomfortable concerning their fear. Once they start to overcome anxiety on this level the lights may be dimmed in the room and then ultimately, after additional sessions, may be shut off. The therapist is there throughout to encourage and support the patient and gain control over the fear. These sessions would advance until the patient feels strong enough to deal with the cause of anxiety independent of the therapist.

Cognitive behavioral therapy can be a very effective with phobias as it attempts to alter the perception of a given phobia by changing the thoughts that trigger the fear.

Neuro-liguistic programming preformed by a hypnotherapist is another possibility whereas the patient can be desensitized by using visualization and body queue's to replace a negative feeling and reaction with a positive, so that the associations that trigger an attack can be removed.

Self hypnotism is available for certain types of fears which allow the individual to interact with a recording and follow the directions that lead to replacing these triggers with a different thought process to derail the fearful reactions. I would not suggest this if your fear is intense or disabling since it is beneficial to be in an observed and controlled environment.

There are literally hundreds of phobias that individuals suffer from. Many of these causes of anxiety are managed using the same or similar treatments. While overcoming the anxiety of a phobia may not be a hundred percent effective in all patients, it certainly lessens the impact of this disabling panic.

OBSESSIVE COMPULSIVE DISORDER

Coping with anxiety of this nature may become more frustrating as this disorder is personalized by the individual's thoughts and environmental compulsions. The symptoms of obsessive compulsive disorder expand to absorb a majority of their waking hours. Many sufferers don't recognize any difference in their behavior at the onset of these anxiety symptoms. As their disorder escalates and their fixations focus on an increased amount of ritualistic behaviors, the cause of anxiety starts to become more relevant. Obsessive compulsive disorder symptoms could resemble but are not limited to any of the following actions:

- Repeats hand washing several times a day for fear of being exposed to germs.
- Feeling the obsession to count items such as steps, ceiling tiles or sidewalk cracks.
- Returns several times to see if they have shut or locked a door.
- Leaving home only to circle the block and return to see if they have shut off the stove or closed the garage door.
- Constantly placing items in order and aligning them to perfection.

As the disorder evolves the individual becomes aware that their behaviors are not rational. Coping with anxieties such as these may become exhausting when it is repeated over and over but even though the individual finds this to be a cause of anxiety, they feel bound to comply with the ritual to fend off feelings of panic or dread.

(Carolyn Chambers, 2006, 30) "To be diagnosed with this disorder, your obsessions and/or compulsions must take up at least one hour every day and interfere with normal routines (for example, if you can't make left turns when driving), occupational functioning, social activities, or relationships. You may feel the need to avoid certain situations. If you're obsessed with cleanliness, you may not be able to use public rest rooms."

The victims of this disorder are not only dealing with their ritualistic actions of checking and rechecking but they are experiencing many thoughts outside of these noticeable compulsions, which become disturbing and troubling to the person. Some tend to view inappropriate sexual images or violent visualizations. The thoughts are random and unwelcome. The person finds it maddening to prevent or attempt to thwart these types of intrusive thoughts.

Researchers cannot locate the exact cause that triggers this disorder and therefore, any noted causes would only be a speculation. A number of treatments are available. Treatments encompass therapies such as cognitive and behavioral therapies. The challenge and difficulty in treating this disorder is to successfully redirect the individual's perception. This is due to the fact that the act of checking and rechecking something is granting the individual temporary relief from the cause of their anxiety, so in essence they are getting satisfaction and reward for their actions.

In an attempt to deprogram obsessive compulsive disorder and decrease some of these anxiety symptoms, the person will be taught to withdrawal from the sensation to recheck the door, or to count their steps, or wash their hands more than once. In many cases anti-anxiety medications may be prescribed.

CHILDHOOD SEPARATION ANXIETY

Childhood separation anxiety can cause anxiety attacks in children due to a psychological condition causing excessive fear and anxiety of separation, loss, or the anxiety of feeling abandoned by a close loved one. The prime example of this is being separated from a parent to whom the individual has a strong emotional attachment that has contributed to ones sense of safety, security and companionship.

Anxiety attacks can develop within the first year of life when a baby and their parents, mostly the mother, develop strong bonds as the baby relies on the mother for not only food and shelter but warmth, love, and security. The baby learns to recognize and link the smell of the mother and the sound of the mother's voice with safety and security over just the first months. This can further manifest itself and interfere with the child's ability to go to bed in a room by themselves where they may feel detached from the safety of the parent. This anxiety attack in children can also produce nightmares of separation as the child is fearful of being alone or abandoned.

If the child is kept secluded from interaction with others this causes anxiety when the mother chooses to leave the baby for a period of time. The parent may find it hard to return to work or simply going shopping for a matter of hours. The child has no reassurance that indicates the mother will return and at this stage does not have any concept of time. This is evident when the baby cannot be satisfied and will cry endlessly. It is important that the child be introduced to a variety of stimulus and multiple individuals at least after a couple of months of growth to lessen the impact or rule out this anxiety.

As the child ages these attacks may become more recognizable if you correlate the changes taking place in their life, with the behaviors they are exhibiting. In some aspects this anxiety is normal as they take steps to enter the world and leave the safety of their parents and home to attend school. Even though the child understands they will be reunited, it is the simple anxiety and fear of being detached from the parent and moving forward alone into the unknown. In some cases the child will refuse to detach themselves from the parent due to extreme fear of this separation.

There may be times when you can take the child to the school and get them to feel more at ease in this environment. The same may be done with riding a bus. If you have city buses available to you it is possible to take a ride and discuss how it will be on the first ride to school, this allows them to attach some form of normalcy to taking a trip on a bus.

This anxiety, until overcome, will prevent an overnight stay at grandma's house or in any other situation that may require the child to be away from home for a night. It is advisable for the adult to use techniques such as sitting to read to the child before leaving the room, leave a small nightlight on, or assure the child that you are right outside the door. Communication is best to resolve these anxieties before they escalate.

When determining a diagnosis of childhood separation anxiety, the health care professional may look at some of the below different symptoms, frequency of occurrence and the length of duration of these episodes.

- Excessive worrying that some event will lead to separation
- Excessive fear about being alone
- Persistent reluctance or refusal to go to sleep
- Recurring distress when separated
- Recurrent nightmares about separation

Children associated with this anxiety may be referred for counseling if they are in an acceptable age range. This will help the child talk out their fears and resolve their insecurities. At the same time the parent learns techniques to help reduce the feelings of these anxieties and ease the child into independence. Behavior modification may also be used in counseling to attempt to alter the way the child views what is causing their anxieties.

As a parent you may want to get a wealth of information to cover different situations and how to help your child cope with their ever changing and growing life. There are books available to help you learn what to look for and how to help your child as they develop. Visit your local bookstore, library or on-line book site.

ADULT SEPARATION ANXIETY

Adult separation anxiety can be relieved by using natural anxiety treatments, such as positive thinking, stress relaxation techniques, and other forms of natural therapy. This anxiety is the same excessive fear and anxiety as child separation anxiety. Of course, the major difference being the age and ability of rational thinking.

The easiest form of adult separation anxiety that most individuals can relate to is the loss of a spouse. During these relationships one spouse sometimes grows totally dependant on the other for companionship, support, and advice. When the threat of losing the spouse is introduced, severe anxiety may be experienced due to the fear and anticipation of the unknown. The dependant partner has built their life around their relationship and imagine their life will have no meaning. They also fear making decisions on their own since they are used to the interaction and feedback of their partner.

Natural anxiety treatments such as learning the steps to positive thinking and stress relaxation techniques will attempt to alter the individual's perception of themselves as an individual person. This will help to focus on their individual strengths and positive qualities that they possess. Positive thinking will enforce the abilities to make responsible independent decisions and how to socialize with other groups of individuals.

For example, in the death of a wife, where the husband has depended on his counterpart for cooking, cleaning, laundry, food shopping, and other similar tasks will doubt his own capabilities in these area since he may have had little to no participation in these activities. The fear of the loneliness and the unknown can be overwhelming given that he is also dealing with the emotions caused by the death of his spouse. The same is true for the wife who fears losing a husband that has always paid the bills and completed the home and car repairs.

The feelings of adult separation can also impact a mother when the last of her children move out of the home. This has also been known as the empty nest syndrome where the last of the children leave the nest and the parent may feel abandoned and lost with the lack of offspring to cater to. After dedicating years to raising a family the mother fears she is inadequate and lacks the skills required to function in the world on this new level of socialization.

If the diagnosis of a health care professional is desired for this form of anxiety the physician will look at the following symptoms, frequency of occurrence and the length of duration of the episodes listed below.

- Excessive worrying about the event such as divorce or death and separation.
- Excessive fear about being alone.
- Recurring distress when separated by their spouse or loved one.
- Excessive worrying about losing the loved one through some unforeseen disaster.
- Recurrent nightmares about separation or loss of the loved one.

When additional help to overcome adult separation anxiety is required, counseling may be appropriately prescribed to help the individual talk out their fears and resolve their insecurities. Behavior modification will also be used in counseling to attempt to alter the individual's perception of what is causing their anxieties. Knowledge and confidence building is a must for this anxiety treatment.

Social Anxiety Disorders

Social anxiety disorders span a wide range of years from anxiety attacks in children to social and speech anxiety in adults. Social anxiety symptoms can be debilitating in all cases. This disorder is a persistent fear of one or more situations in which the person is exposed to possible scrutiny by others and fears that he or she may do something or act in a way that will be humiliating or embarrassing.

The anxiety symptoms may vary in intensity and duration. This disorder exceeds normal shyness or discomfort in social situations. It may lead to excessive social avoidance and substantial social or occupational impairment. An attack can trigger a fight or flight response associated with any stressful situation. Once threatened to be placed in a social or center of attention situation, the immediate response is to look for an escape route. Many people are nervous or self conscious from time to time but social anxiety disorders cause an intense fear as the person anticipates being judged and condemned by others so bad, that this interferes with their everyday functioning and what would be considered a normal interaction or routine.

Although hard to define, this disorder can start with the early formation of social functioning. Anxiety attacks in children that are overlooked or misdiagnosed may advance to a more serious level. Enhanced symptoms could trigger a reaction of speech anxiety that may be severe enough for the child to cease verbal communication. This is a reaction used to protect them from being humiliated and/or negatively evaluated. Adults in extreme cases could turn to seclusion to avoid all interaction with others.

It's normal to have some amount of speech anxiety before giving a speech, it's not normal to avoid getting a college degree because you know it would be impossible for you to take a required speech class. It's normal to feel anxious when having to go to a social function where you may not know other people that will be attending. It's a social anxiety disorder if you worry for days, weeks, or months rehashing your fear of the upcoming event. It's normal at times to feel self conscious but it's not normal when you refuse to eat in front of other people or feel you are being watched and judged by everyone around you.

Look for symptoms such as, a child who experiences extreme distress over every day activities like playing with others or is uncomfortable and fearful of answering questions in front of classmates. Other symptoms in children or adults may be an avoidance of eye contact, shaky voice, sweating, trembling or shaking, flushed face, or clammy hands. Symptoms not so noticeable by others would include; fast heartbeat, hot flashes, upset stomach, muscle tension, dry mouth or the mind drawing a blank when asked to speak.

Some triggers that may contribute to social anxiety disorder could be:

- Meeting new people
- Being the center of attention
- Being observed while doing something
- Making small talk
- Public speaking
- Performing on stage
- Being teased or criticized
- Talking with authority figures
- Being called on in class
- Going on a date
- Making phone calls
- Using public bathrooms
- Taking exams
- Eating and drinking in public
- Speaking up in a meeting or attending social functions

Therapy tends to be the same as for working with phobias since these are of close relation. Cognitive behavioral therapy may be used to act out, role play or visualize the events that create tension. This is an attempt to alter the perception of a given phobia by changing the thoughts that trigger the fear.

Only after the initial phobia is under control can group therapy be suggested. Some people feel they are alone with this disorder but the truth is that many individuals suffer from social anxiety disorder. The knowledge and exchange of information is very beneficial to gain confidence and learn how others approached and conquered or are working at conquering this fear.

CHAPTER 3
VERBAL ABUSE / MENTAL STRESS

(Mayo Clinic) "Strong stress reactions sometimes can be traced to early environmental factors. People who were exposed to extremely stressful events as children, such as neglect or abuse, tend to be particularly vulnerable to stress as adults."

Many individuals suffer from the effects of abusive relationships, past and present that is why this issue should be looked at very closely for identifying issues of anxiety, self esteem, and insecurities. An abuser is an individual who uses tactics such as threats, humiliation, domination, intimidation, terrorization, and even physical abuse of another person to hold control over their victim. Verbal abuse is one of the strongest forms of mental stress especially in impressionable years when self esteem is being developed. This is where many disorders start their origination.

There are many causes of verbal abuse. Many child abusers may well have been victims of abuse themselves. Mental illness is another common factor, with many abusers suffering with personality disorders or other severe forms of mental illness. Parental choices and other unforeseen circumstances that place families under extraordinary stress such as, poverty, divorce, sickness, disability, lack of parental skills, or alcohol and drugs are often associated with child maltreatment. Many of these factors may contribute to family stress that can result in child abuse or neglect.

Morgan never had seen her father much after five years of age. She remembers over the years her mothers constant taunting of saying, "You need to lose weight," "Suck in your stomach," "Hold your breath," "Nobody could ever want you," "You are so stupid," "You'll never amount to anything," "You're useless." She reflects on her feelings of abandonment, "She stopped tucking us in and saying I love you, shortly after leaving my father. There wasn't too much loving interaction after that."

It was when Morgan was a teenager, that all of the years she assumed her father had not wanted anything to do with her that she found out the truth. Her father had sent cards over the years and gifts and even called, but every time he attempted to contact Morgan or her sister he was blocked by Morgan's mother. Cards and gifts were discarded, phone calls never made it to the girls and when they brought up the topic of their father it was swiftly kicked to the curb with statements that he had his own life to live now and he didn't want to be bothered by them.

It was eventually a somewhat happy ending when the girls found out that he really did care and he was eager to see them. Then they made it a point to open communications with their dad on a regular basis and each year they would drive out of state together to go to visit with him for a few days. Whenever it became time to say their goodbyes and drive away, Morgan would always look back at him standing there in the driveway. He would always have tears in his eyes and her heart would be breaking. She believed that they both grieved over the lost years of love that they missed.

(Bradshaw, 1988, [b] 94) "Children who need their parents time, attention and direction for at least 15 years, do not get it. They are abandoned. Since the children need their parents all the time, and since they do not get their needs met, they grow with a cup that has a hole in it. This hole in the soul is the fuel that drives the compulsivity. The person looks for more and more love, attention, praise, booze, money, etc."

A lot of the time Morgan felt that her mother didn't want to be bothered with her or her sister. "We were in the way," she says. "She hardly let that stop her. She worked all day and spent the evenings drinking with her boyfriend/husband and wandered in after the bars closed. My sister and I were pretty much on our own from an age that truly needed stricter supervision," Morgan admits. "Since she didn't spend enough time in our lives as a mother she found she couldn't use discipline, it became easier to look the other way or just accept what was happening. She gave me permission to smoke at age 14 since she knew telling me "no" wouldn't change anything and I was pregnant at age 15 as I searched for the love to fill the large void in my heart."

If your parents only verbally recognized you any time that you did something they were not pleased with then they were limiting your development and growth of your self-esteem. You may have been repeatedly told things such as you were stupid, ugly, fat, or worthless, or a choice of many other abusive words such as Morgan experienced. When continuously being told these things year after year, over and over, you come to believe and accept these flaws in yourself as true. They must be correct since you have tried everything to make things better, to do things right and nothing worked and nothing changed.

Morgan recalls covering her head and rocking back and forth on her bed to try to drown out the sounds of yelling and loud crashes. This was a regular occurrence when her mother returned home with her male companion after a night of drinking. This brings to mind the first time at age thirteen when she couldn't handle it any more and with gathered bravery rose from bed and interrupted a fight. This was the first time in her life she considers that she had used foul language. "When I entered the kitchen I seen my mother lying on the floor with a size 10 ½ shoe pressed against her head as he threatened to kill her. Full of pure anger I yelled at him saying, "Get the hell out of here." He didn't want to deal with my confrontation so he left. As he tried to get away and out the door I had to pull my mother back as she went crying after him, begging him to come back. Little did I know at the time, that my mother would condemn me for my action."

So many times the abuser will take advantage of the state of mind of his victim and convince them that they are not good enough, or worthy enough to deserve someone to love them. Convinced of those thoughts the victim feels that if this person escapes them, their life will be meaningless. This places the victim in the state of helplessness. Their desperation is so intense that they would rather live with the abuse no matter how physical, than to live with nothing.

Mental stress caused by verbal abuse leaves scars but they are scars buried deep inside. They are kept hidden from and protected from onlookers. Individuals may experience feelings of helplessness when they place the blame on themselves for what has occurred in their life. The victim feels personally responsible for the bad decisions and the paths that they may have chosen to take in the past. The one thing the victim has to be reminded of is the fact that, whatever choices were made appeared to be the right choice at that particular time and place, they did not intentionally make a bad decision. The victim is not responsible to foresee the future. We all make bad choices at times but if we stop making choices, we stop living.

(Bradshaw, 1988, [b] 5) "Our families are the places where we have our source of relationships. Families are where we first learn about ourselves in the mirroring eyes of our parents, where we see ourselves for the first time. In families we learn about emotional intimacy. We learn what feelings are and how to express them. Our parents model what feelings are acceptable and family authorized and what feelings are prohibited."

When parents neglect or abuse their children mentally or physically by not showing affection such as being held, touched, or nurtured, the grown adult finds it difficult to relate to touch and may not know how to respond to such actions. They become tense and may instinctively withdraw by physically pulling away from the situation.

After frequent and lengthy subjection to mental stress the child may have chosen to react by not reacting. They have learned that what they say will be incorrect and consequently choose not to speak. To keep from being recognized they will keep a distance from others and avoid eye contact.

By keeping their self isolated they are protecting themselves from all mental stress leading to pain and emotion connected to rejection. With mental stress as a child the emotionally abused child learns to disconnect themselves from their emotions as a means of self preservation. In doing this they block their feelings and are unable to show any emotion. These individuals are often viewed in their adult life as being cold or uncaring.

They may develop an obsession of trying to please others and always fall short of their own expectations. When in the years where relationships begin to flourish they may search for someone to love them. This can also manifest into an obsession and again they may always fall short, never feeling the love that they so much crave.

Sometimes due to the fear of rejection from prior years riveted with mental stress they enter an abusive relationship because this is a comfort zone they have become accustomed to, treading unfamiliar ground is thought only to bring rejection. They feel they are not good enough or worthy enough to expect anything better so they don't even try. (Jampolsky, 1979, 53) "When we expect others to satisfy our desires, and they disappoint us, as they inevitably must, we then experience distress. This distress can take the form of frustration, disappointment, anger, depression or illness." Inevitably these abusive relationships also do not last. This only enforces the feeling of rejection as the individual retreats back to the safety of isolation. Loneliness will play a large part with emotionally abused individuals due to this isolation.

"Yes," Morgan agrees, "I began to follow my mothers footsteps, bars were a type of comfortable atmosphere for me. My sister and I spent many hours as children tagging along with my mother since she probably didn't know what else to do with us and I'm sure there must have been a slight guilt for not spending enough time with us. I was able to get served by the bartenders since I was 15 years old as long as I visited the bar with my mother, why wouldn't I follow that path? As my sister grew she found content in reading many books and her path led to the lord who she has maintained her loyalty with over the years. I on the other hand, began to find my escape through alcohol. This of course, led me to spend all my free time at a bar. I chose at the time, to become attached to alcoholics that were mentally and physically abusive. I still never found satisfaction. I could never feel the love inside that I craved, expected or needed."

"As strange as it may be," Morgan says "when another is abusing to someone who is in a state of helplessness, the victim still acknowledges this as a form of attention, and since they crave attention this becomes acceptable. At times, in these forms of relationships the victim may even provoke an occurrence when actually what they truly want is affection. It is a normal response from this type of abuser to wake up the following morning and cry for forgiveness, promising over and over again that this will never reoccur…. and he is forgiven. This lasts a day or two before the vicious cycle starts over."

"We will repeatedly tell ourselves that the beatings are our fault and we will work so hard every day in the attempt to make him happy. The positive reinforcement that the abuser receives is one reason why he will always be an abuser. As long as he can maintain control over our mental state he knows that we will remain dependant on him. Our other feelings of entrapment stem from our knowledge that we have nowhere else to go, there is nothing to go back to."

(Bradshaw, 1988, [b] 88) "As paradoxical as it seems, many a child of an alcoholic becomes an alcoholic. And if they don't become an alcoholic, they marry an alcoholic or a person with some other compulsive addictive personality disorder."

Social settings always leave the emotionally abused person feeling left out. They are afraid to communicate for fear of rejection. This is an extension of social anxiety behavior from childhood causing a persistent fear. This person fears that he or she may do something or act in a way that will be humiliating or embarrassing. This makes them feel that they are an outsider always looking in but never being able to become involved. This behavior is sometimes misinterpreted as stuck up and conceited. Others perceive that this person believes that they are better than anyone else and as a result keep their distance. Ironic how our perception can be the very opposite of fact yet we choose to believe the illusion.

If you find that you were mentally abused then it is now time to face those facts and accept how you were abused. Accept the fact that this left wounds that need to be healed emotionally. You will learn that there is a need to forgive and to let go of all of those negative emotions of betrayal or hatred, you can't carry this baggage with you into the future. You need to accept the pain knowing that you are going to feel it with all of your heart and then place it behind you so that you can advance forward with your life.

There will come a point in your life when you become distanced enough from your abusers that you reach a breaking point. When this happens you will accept that it is now *you* who is the director of your life, *you* can now create your own reality. When you reach this point in your life where you want to place all of these insecurities behind you, changing your perception will be the key to your future. You will accept the experiences that you have had and then choose to move forward with a new and more accurate assessment of what life has to offer you.

Morgan reflected on her first enormous step forward. "I realized that I wanted to live a better life and try to give my son a life away from violence. When this happened, although I was still living with an abuser, I had slowly branched out and started to read self help books. I always kept them tucked in the back of a drawer but over time I gained strength from these books. One day I had gathered enough bravery to tell my abuser that I wanted out of our relationship. To make a long story short, he decided to move back to his home state. The day he was leaving, as I was standing in the kitchen of my apartment, he took his last suitcase to the door, looked back and said, "Once I walk out this door you will never see or hear from me again." I looked him straight in the eyes and very calmly said, "Goodbye." When the door closed I felt many emotions but the strongest emotion was a feeling of liberation. I finally did it and I had no clue as to how I was going to move forward from here but I had a roof over my head and a job to pay the bills… the rest would come, I had faith."

(Carolyn Chambers, 2006, 170) "Because you may have been abused or neglected in your family of origin, you may abuse or neglect yourself. The key to elevating your esteem is the willingness to take responsibility for your thoughts, feelings, or actions. On the surface you may think you want to succeed, but when you have low self esteem, old messages you learned in your family continue to operate. These messages are like tapes playing in your head. They're faulty because they have nothing to do with you and everything to do with the person who gave you the message."

Mental health practices such as psychotherapy or psychiatry are very encouraging with their progress to help individuals deal with mental abuse and may be a choice of therapy to help strengthen your self esteem and build your confidence. It is also beneficial to overcome any emotional turmoil that you are unable to come to terms with while you are in a controlled setting. You exchange conversation with a professional who is able to be objective and offer many alternatives to help you to move through your pain and thus enable you to move forward with your life. Your family physician should be able to recommend a reputable specialist to help you.

Morgan remembers her favorite psychologist, Ms. Ebalo, "Although I never showed emotions, I also found that I could never verbalize anything about my past, within the first sentence I was overwhelmed with tears and would have to stop talking to pull myself back together. So talk on this subject was nonexistent with anyone for many years of my life. Ms. Ebalo, after our first visit had me go home with an assignment to complete, write a letter to my mother, one that she assured me nobody would ever see, not even her. I was to bring it back on my next visit. Within this letter I was to write my true feelings as harsh as they may have been at the time. On my next visit she had me read the letter out loud. Wow, that was difficult and I had to stop many times to regain control when my words wouldn't come but she reassured me to try to relax and take my time. I think it took the full session to get all the words from that letter out of my mouth but she knew that if I couldn't speak that I could write. She also knew that I needed to accomplish getting these feelings verbalized to turn them into a reality to be dealt with, this was my second enormous step forward."

There are two questions I must ask of you at this point.

1. Are you holding the controls in your life?

2. What is holding you back from the things that you would like to accomplish with your life?

These answers can start you on the road to discovery. These are hurdles that cannot block your path. You need to take your power back to be in control of your own life. Identify the barriers and make plans to overcome them.

CHAPTER 4
BRINGING OUR BODIES IN BALANCE

Balance is a matter of learning to stabilize the different parts of your life so that they all work together smoothly. We all have had circumstances where we have left work after we have experienced a frustrating day and we couldn't wait to get home to rant and rave as we bounced some of these frustrations off of another as a sounding board. This on occasion is normal. It becomes a problem when you carry your work home more than just occasionally and it cuts into the time that is meant to be used for your family, spouse and relaxation time. The same can happen in reverse where you are continuously getting personal calls at work and your supervisor has a problem with you spending hours on the phone handling personal issues when you should be productive in your job. Balance also needs to be stabilized with your health, proper nutrition and sleep when it comes to developing a healthy lifestyle. When any one of these functions is out of balance, it resembles a domino effect that overlaps into an area of your life, then that imbalance overflows into another area of your life and so on.

Imagine for a moment what your life would be like if it was balanced. You would see the smooth transition between tasks, the peaceful interaction with your family, friend or spouse, feeling healthy with a clear mind, no longer finding that you are exhausted as you drag yourself through the day. Your surroundings are organized and you carry this sense of calmness inside of you that allows you to react to any situation with composure as you remain relaxed and at ease in your surroundings. Yes, this is actually possible!

If your body is constantly responding to a high degree of stress, you may be more vulnerable to life-threatening health problems. In today's fast pace world creating balance in your life is an important aspect of staying healthy. Many illnesses have been found to be stress related. Depending on how these symptoms of stress present themselves in your life, they can turn into full-blown illnesses without warning.

When seeking to bring balance into your life to defeat stress our physical health will always be part of the equation and requires balance just as our emotional and mental health. The primary needs of our body's health are in relation to nutrition and what we put into our bodies, sleep that rejuvenates both our physical and mental well being, and physical fitness that keeps our body at peak performance.

NUTRITION

*The **second** key habit to avoid when attempting to reduce stress that may cause us even more stress and cause damage to our health is compulsive eating.*

Eating *- The stress of being overweight causes you to eat. / When you eat you get stressed about being overweight. / So you eat more.*

(Elizabeth Scott, M.S.) "There are several ways in which stress can contribute to weight gain. Whether we're stressed because of constant, crazy demands at work or we're really in danger, our bodies respond like we're about to be harmed and need to fight for our lives. To answer this need, we experience a burst of energy, shifts in metabolism and blood flow, and other changes. If you remain in this state for a prolonged amount of time due to chronic stress, your health becomes at risk. Aside from a host of other dangers, chronic stress can also cause weight gain."

When some individuals become stressed, they may experience a nervous energy that causes them to turn to eating in an attempt to keep themselves occupied and relieve their stressful thoughts. When in this state of mind they can munch down a whole bag of chips and a box of donuts, then wash it down with a couple of cola drinks. Even while performing this ritual, these individuals know that it is a self defeating behavior and they will not be happy once they have stopped eating and look back at the calories they have devoured, but they crave the temporary fix so the cycle continues.

Nutrition not only fuels the body but it fuels the mind. I guess the "you are what you eat" saying does have some merit to it. When you eat healthy items such as fruits, vegetables, and legumes you are pumping vitamins, minerals, and proteins through your body which also contributes to a healthy mind. If you are filling your food cravings with pastries, chocolate, and grease these empty calories are weighing both your body and your mind down as you lose energy and become weak.

Eating is one of our bodies natural support systems used to rejuvenate our energy and keep us healthy. One of the most problematic issues associated with stress is poor nutrition. If your stress is causing bad eating habits, then you can fall into one of two categories: you are over indulging by eating high-fat, high-calorie foods, or you are finding that you just can't eat at all, meaning your body is getting improper nutrition. If you are over indulging then as your weight increases, so will your stress level. If you are not eating, you will fall ill and this will trigger an increase in your stress. Either path is harmful and self-destructive. Balance in nutrition means eating regularly as well as eating healthy foods that energize the body and mind. Bad nutritional habits can trigger a chain reaction that will deteriorate your health as well as amplify your stress.

You first need to determine what the triggers are that cause you to reach for those high fat, high calorie foods. A trigger is any situation that prompts your mind to revert to a specific behavior based on past habits. This can be based on visual stimulus or activity. These types of triggers will attempt to weaken your willpower and therefore, need to be modified or eliminated from your environment. Focus on identifying and then reducing your personal triggers.

We sometimes tend to eat for more reasons than to just sustain life. We eat when we are stressed, bored, depressed, lonely, or just have a case of low self esteem, among other obvious reasons like being hungry. Food can become a comforting blanket wrapped around us to cover many underlying issues that need resolution. Too many high fat foods will slow our bodies down rather than energize them. Weight gain could escalate to obesity when no corrective actions are taken to control the stress. We continue on roller coaster rides of diets and when each fails, because we never truly change our eating patterns, our stress increases, our willpower decreases, and depression and negative thinking take control of your mind and body as you reach for that cheese danish.

(Dr. Melvyn Kinder, 1990, 107) "From the time our mothers tucked in our shirts and made us comb our hair before visiting relatives, we learned that it was important to look just right. We inferred that if it's important to look your best, then the better we look, the greater the social value. Sure, we also learned that wonderful maxim "beauty" is in the eyes of the beholder, but we came to suspect that the "beholder" still expected us to look our best."

Morgan still suffers from the delusion today that she has never been pretty enough or thin enough. She has never been able to overcome the haunting voice of the past that continues to say, "Suck in your stomach," "Hold your breath," "Nobody could ever want you," "You need to lose weight," over and over it was reinforced by her mother's words that she was unattractive. She may never conquer these issues with her image but she admits she has gotten much better over the years.

Perception plays a dramatic role in this topic. When we watch television we are flooded with images of perfection. Women receive the impression that they need to be thin to be pretty. Men are projected to be more attractive with bulging muscles and six pack abs. Our culture places such a high importance on physical attraction that most of us have expectations that we will never be able to live up to concerning our physical appearance. Losing weight is one thing, seeing absolute perfection in the mirror is another.

What we fail to think of, is that we are looking at actors and actresses that are fighting to maintain a certain *correct* image. They earn large sums of money and can spend a large amount of their time in the gym. They hire nutritionists and personal trainers to help them stay on track and motivated. If this doesn't work for them, they have the income to seek help from the medical field, with plastic surgeons who will perform liposuctions, facelifts, tummy tucks, nose jobs, or a number of other cosmetic alterations. Then before they go on screen, professionals who do their makeup cover any left over imperfections they may have, to make them appear flawless.

If it is this type of look you are striving for, you are doing so in vain. This is a distortion of perfection, not reality. To try to compete with this sort of image is ludicrous. Nutrition and dieting is a balance that creates a healthy body and mind. You may want to set your goals for perfection high enough to keep you motivated, but believing you will actually attain perfectionism is setting yourself up for failure. This is a sure way of continuing an unhealthy cycle of starvation and binge eating.

Now that you have a basic understanding of the downfalls of stress as it pertains to nutrition, let's focus on what needs to be done to get you on a path of proper nutritional habits. Always keep in the forefront of your mind that life is about choices and the choices you make today, will most certainly dictate the paths you will follow tomorrow.

When you are dealing with any weight issues you need to become aware of the foods that you choose and the amount of fat content that they contain. Look to the labels prior to purchasing them to see the calorie count per serving size. Steer away from items that contain more than one third of their calorie count in fat calories. Follow the example below when making your food choices.

COUNTING FAT FROM GRAMS TO CALORIES

Take the amount of fat grams listed on the label and multiply that number by 9. This should equal no more than one third, or 33 percent, of the total calories per serving number.

Example: Total calories for a serving size of rice snack cakes (9 cakes) are 70, while the total fat grams are 2.5 per serving then (2.5 x 9 = 23)

The total fat calories in 9 cakes are 23, which mean that 23 calories should be less than one third of the total calories, 70. The easiest way would be to take 23 x 3; you don't want that amount to go over 70. It equals 69 and therefore is a good snack item.

Remember, you can't have a bag of forty-five cakes, which would then equal the amount of 350 calories. That would be considered a meal, and a poor nutritional meal I may add. If portions seem to be your downfall and you are trying to reduce the amount of calories that you intake, you may want to consider having a TV dinner a couple of evenings a week.

Evening time is where stress ends its day with a bang! You may decide that you deserve all of this food and relaxation after the day of stress you have had to contend with. Beware this is when you should be concentrating on eating your light meal, since you will be less likely to work it off prior to going to bed. If you are looking to lighten your calorie intake during the day, then selecting soup for lunch with a couple of crackers could be one of your options. Eating a heavy lunch filled with pasta, may give you a spurt of energy but it will make you tired later, which will add to the stress of your day's activities. Be sure to remember to keep healthy in mind when picking up something ready to eat or using a delivery service.

It's hard to control the hunger when you never seem to feel full, but with plenty of low fat cooking tips this is certainly not impossible. Reducing fat content and controlling portions, along with physical fitness, are the keys to losing weight and balancing mind and body. The following are helpful tips that you can use to curb your hunger and assist with changing your eating habits.

Drink Water - Water is an essential part of our body. Water will flush toxins from your body as well as replenish your fluids when you are dehydrated. Don't drink water only when you feel thirsty. Our bodies crave liquids, and we often misinterpret our body's signal that we are thirsty as hunger. This is one of the easiest ways to satisfy some of your cravings and the need to occupy your hands with activity. If you eliminate the need your body has for fluids, you may automatically find yourself eating less.

Flavor your Foods - Use seasonings to flavor your foods. Weight gain can be fueled by those tastes of foods with high fat content that you trained your mind by repetition to crave. Start by preparing some low fat meals that are easy and convenient on the week days which are usually busy days. Then on the week-ends, you can have a little more time to play in the kitchen and you can experiment with combinations of foods and spices. What's even more entertaining with stress reducing benefits, is getting your partner involved sharing ideas and helping with preparation.

Eat Lots of Vegetables - One very important way to stay healthy is to increase your intake of vegetables at every meal. These are not only good for you and help to fill you up, but they are also low in calories and something we can never seem to get enough of. Vegetables are best if steamed to maintain the highest nutritional value, but if steaming is not an option then baking is your second best, then boiling. When you are selecting vegetables, it is better to use fresh rather than canned or frozen.

Keep your Fat Intake Low - Keep your intake of fat, and especially saturated fat, low. Daily intake of fat should only equal one third of your daily calorie intake to create a healthy balance and proper nutrition. Saturated fat found in the high-fat content meats and dairy products is the worst fat that we can consume. Our intake of these products should be limited.

Eat Proper Levels of Food at each Mealtime - Eat the bulk of your calories at breakfast and lunch so you have the energy you need to make it through the day. Most individuals may find it easier to eat less through these periods of the day since their mind is occupied on many other tasks, but eating more at night won't offer you the same opportunity to work it off.

Don't Skip Meals - One of the first and most important rules in proper nutrition is not to skip any meals. This of course is easier said than done when you are trying to couple eating right and losing weight at the same time, but monitoring what you eat is as essential as eating on a regular basis. Breakfast is the most important meal of the day because it helps get your metabolism going. You have over time already established that when you skip a meal such as lunch, you are famished by the time dinner has arrived and this makes it almost impossible to make smart decisions. This can easily lead to eating twice as much just because of the desperate feelings of hunger you are experiencing.

Drink with Moderation -You don't need to eliminate coffee, soda, tea, or alcoholic beverages from your life, but at least make the commitment to cut down on your intake of these drinks. Above all, try to avoid consuming any stimulants during the evening hours if you have trouble sleeping at night.

The **third** key habit to avoid when attempting to reduce stress that may cause us even more stress and cause damage to our health is excessive drinking of alcohol.

Alcohol – Being stressed causes you to drink. / Drinking causes stress. / So you drink more.

(The HART-Empire) "Large alcohol consumption stimulates the hypothalamus, pituitary and adrenal glands. One result is an increase in the amount of cortisol produced within the body. Another is an increase in adrenaline. Both of those, while they don't alone cause stress, play a large role in the symptoms. Extreme stress makes it more difficult to concentrate. One of the obvious effects of high alcohol intake is to produce that exact effect. Thus, heavy drinkers get a double whammy just at the moment they need mental clarity most."

Make three lists - You can continue to make modifications to your foods by using proper nutritional knowledge to eliminate a high fat content food for a more nutritional choice. The three lists will contain food that you like, with two restrictions to the list, the food must be both healthy and low calorie. One list needs to contain foods that you may enjoy for breakfast, one for lunch and one list for dinner. If you have a lack of imagination, buy a small calorie counter book. This lists foods you may not have considered which will increase your list choices. Remember, this tool is a calorie counter, it doesn't mean that everything listed is good for you or low in calories, it simply gives you a wide range of foods and their calorie count.

Recruit a Friend – Teaming up with someone else that also has the desire to lose weight and get healthy has multiple benefits. You will have someone to walk with, go to the gym with, or do other exercises with as well as someone to help keep you motivated. You may both decide to join a weight loss program together, and a little healthy competition to see who loses more is always a good strategy.

Take a supplemental vitamin -Vitamins are essential for a well balanced diet and also aid our bodies by contributing to the proper nutrition that they need on a daily basis. There are vitamins directly linked to Stress relief as well as daily multi-vitamins available on the market. If in doubt of a reputable multi-vitamin ask the pharmacist at your local drug store.

(Ross, 2002, 93) "You'll need all of the basic nutrients and then some, to make up for what you've lost to past stress and poor diet. For example, your adrenals (glands) use up about 90 percent of the vitamin C you take in and require a constant rich supply of the B vitamins as well. Your basic calcium, magnesium, and vitamin D are also used up at a tremendous rate by your adrenals during stress. Your adrenals need plenty of both vitamin D and omega-3 fat in order to make their stress-fighting adrenaline and norepinephrine. Many people report significantly increased energy as well as peace of mind when they take these two nutrients as part of their basic supplements."

Exercise -This isn't so bad if you choose to do something that you enjoy. Proper nutrition isn't all about what we put into our bodies but the balance that we incorporate between food and fitness. Go for long walks (nature walks are great if you have any within close proximity to your location). Working in the yard is both visually rewarding and physical. It also gives your mind time to relax, which aids in reducing the pressures and stress that may be one of your triggers to eating.

Keep your self busy - One of the biggest triggers to eating is television. This can be the hardest to master simply due to the commercials every 10 minutes showing you pictures of tempting foods and weakening your will power. Keeping your hands busy with a hobby or craft helps immensely to redirect your attention during those dreaded commercials. Simply focus all of your attention to whatever you're working on knowing that, this too shall pass. (See relaxation techniques to locate some possible hobby choices.)

Pamper Yourself - Another satisfying diversion technique to keep you focused *off* food and focused *on* proper nutrition is to pamper yourself, have a portable single CD player, candle or diffuser, and bubble bath on hand at all times. Take the time you deserve to spoil yourself. Run a warm bubble bath; place a candle or diffuser on the counter and a relaxation tape in the CD. Let the warm water sooth and relax every muscle. Wrap yourself in a comfortable bathrobe when done and curl up to read a good book.

Avoidance - Of course, you know the biggest taboo - don't keep high fat snacks and food in your house. This only weakens your willpower more if you should start to waiver. Having to make a special trip to the store may deter you long enough to get your mind back on track with the use of one of your other diversion techniques.

By learning to work with the body instead of against it, you can ignite your natural fat-burning furnace and reprogram your body to burn fat and keep it off for good. Simply put, eat the right foods and send instructions of weight loss and health; eat the wrong foods and send messages of weight gain and disease.

Below are some nutritional tips for low fat cooking that will give you some ideas for slowly incorporating change and a healthy balance into your lifestyle during every meal. Incorporating these low fat cooking tips into your normal routine meal choices will assist in giving your body the proper nutrition that it needs, while cutting fat calories from your food content. Add these new choices to your weekly shopping list.

LOW FAT COOKING TIPS

√ Use an egg substitute rather than whole eggs.

√ Use a low-fat spray such as Pam rather than butter or margarine, or use olive oil.

√ Choose lean meats and replace ground beef with ground turkey.

√ Replace whole milk with no more than 2% milk.

√ Flavor foods using onions, sweet peppers, garlic, paprika, pepper, basil, parsley, or Worcestershire sauce.

√ Use mustard or no-fat mayo on your sandwich rather than mayonnaise or salad dressing.

√ Replace sugar with honey when you are able.

√ Use marinara sauce rather than a thick paste spaghetti sauce.

√ Use whole wheat pasta and choose brown rice over white rice.

√ Choose sweet potatoes over white potatoes for most occasions.

√ When you select white potatoes, cook them by steaming, baking, or boiling. You may want to sprinkle with some fresh parsley on top.

√ Use a chicken broth to flavor mashed potatoes rather than milk and butter.

√ Have a tossed salad available at every evening meal. Use romaine lettuce or a mixture of lettuce. This will give you a higher amount of nutritional benefit. Mix a three-bean salad or mix mandarin oranges and sliced apple pieces in with your greens to give added zest. Select a low-fat salad dressing or use a balsamic vinaigrette.

√ When it comes to bread, select whole wheat or whole grain. Additional nutritional tips for the morning would be to choose, bagels, English muffins, oatmeal, bran muffin, or a cereal containing whole wheat or bran is preferable. Any choice of cereal containing high fiber or grain is your best alternative.

√ Vegetables are a good filler and full of vitamins. Try to use as many fresh vegetables as you can. Again, as stated in the potatoes nutritional tip, steaming is your best alternative for cooking. Some good choices are Brussels sprouts, peas, sweet red peppers, carrots, squash, artichokes, spinach, broccoli, cucumber, celery, tomatoes, cabbage, asparagus, string beans, beets, cauliflower, and beans such as kidney, pinto, or navy.

√ Fruits are excellent to snack on in between meals. Apples, bananas, watermelon, strawberries, oranges, mangos, cherries, cantaloupe, honeydew, pears, peaches, grapefruit, tangerines and grapes are all good, nutritious, and low in calories.

√ Select fish, turkey, Cornish hen, or chicken without skin as the main part of your meal.

√ Applesauce is a healthy and low calorie filler with any meal.

√ When you look for desserts or snacks other than fruit, consider items like yogurt, raisins, pretzels, Jell-o, rice cakes, popcorn, bagel chips or a frozen yogurt.

Also remember, if you need to drastically change your eating habits and also suffer from a health condition, you should first speak to your medical practitioner or a registered dietitian for any particular guidelines that may pertain to your specific condition. These professionals can be of great assistance when dealing with particular illnesses and dietary needs.

Whether you go it alone or with the assistance of a dietician, make small adjustments and commitments to eliminate high-fat unhealthy foods from your diet over a period of time. Commit to one change and then add another selection after you have conquered the first. Make changes you know you will stick with. When incorporating proper nutrition into your lifestyle, keep in mind that you must permanently change your eating habits for good nutrition to be effective. You will not only make your body feel healthy but you will have a more positive outlook and attitude in general when you feel healthy and strong.

There are other options to assist you in losing weight and keeping your motivation high such as self hypnosis. This doesn't consist of visits to a hypnotherapist it consists of listening to a CD that when listened to often will keep you on track until you can reach your goals then keep you there. (more on hypnosis later)

SLEEP

---

*The **fourth** key* habit to avoid when attempting to reduce stress that may cause us even more stress and cause damage to our health is taking sleeping pills.

Sleeping Pills – *Stress causes sleep disorders. / You take sleeping pills which can cause side effects that produce stress which can cause sleep disorders. / So you take more sleeping pills.*

(Chantel Alise, eHow Editor) "Nearly 60 percent of all Americans report problems with insomnia that range from occasional to chronic. The reasons behind the bouts, however, vary significantly. Some of the most common causes include work-related stress, family-related stress, financial concerns, problems with anger, depression, mood swings, illness and other problems."

If you are ever prescribed sleeping pills, make yourself aware of the side effects of the particular pill that you are taking. All sleeping pills have side effects which may consist of dizziness, fatigue, night sweats, headache, sluggishness during waking hours, nausea, upper respiratory infections, joint and muscle pain, muscle cramps, convulsions, tremors, feeling of being hung over, an inability to concentrate, anxiety, loss of appetite, constipation, dry mouth or an unusual taste in the mouth, skin rash, thoughts of suicide, uncontrolled aggression, hallucinations, behavioral changes, depression, and even worsened insomnia.

Just as eating is one of our bodies natural support systems used to rejuvenate our energy and keep us healthy, our other important function to health, especially mental health is sleep. Sleep not only gives your body renewed energy but gives your mind a well needed break in the day's events. Not getting the proper sleep can leave you vulnerable to contracting illnesses that your body would have normally had the ability to defend itself against. This means that proper sleep also needs to be balanced to avoid feeling fatigued, but what happens when stress overtakes our life and sleep is hard to come by?

When we are experiencing acute stress such as worrying about starting a new job, we may find that a temporary disruptive problem occurs with our sleep patterns. With chronic stress you may be leaning more towards insomnia when these episodes are prolonged and go unattended. (Michael Castleman, 2000, 296) "Insomnia's cost extends beyond the bedroom. Compared to normal sleepers, people with insomnia are less productive at work and have twice as many auto accidents. They also report generally poorer health, because sleep is critical to immune function." If you are experiencing any problems getting rest at night, you should bring this to the attention of your family physician so that an assessment can be made to rule out any serious health issues.

With a reduced amount of time to rejuvenate your mind and body you may feel that the next day you are less tolerant of activities that would not normally have a negative effect on you. Exhaustion and low energy will make you drowsy and unable to focus on the days tasks. This can disrupt not only your relationships with the people you love, but it can effect how you are perceived in your place of employment. Your lack of sleep can influence your mood which in turn will influence how you react in a stressful situation.

(Gail C. Mornhinweg, Ph.D., R.N.) A recent study by Gail C Mornhinweg, PhD found that music can help you sleep better and deeper. On the nights when they listened to relaxing music before going to bed, all participants in the study except one reported falling asleep faster and sleeping longer than normal. Interestingly, most also reported that sleeplessness returned on the nights that they did not listen to music.

One of the ways I use to get a good nights rest is better than sliced bread... I know "what can be better than that!!" It is called a **digital stereo pillow speaker.** Wow, is this fantastic and believe me I have struggled for years. I was a little hesitant at first, not knowing how you would be able to hear through the pillow but with the combination of the speakers (which are inserted in a foam protection) and the pillows fibers, it's like you're transported into your own world. You can use any relaxation CD that you wish but the CD that I received with mine is outstanding.

If unhealthy sleep patterns persist it can lead to many negative affects on your mental and physical health, these are listed below:

- Health problems
- Make you irritable
- Slow your performance
- You cannot hold your concentration
- You feel fatigued
- May cause memory problems
- Can decrease your reaction time which can lead to vehicle crashes when on the road
- Hinders the rebuilding and strengthening of your immune system
- Can lead to depression

Usually, you will find that there is an underlying issue contributing to your restless nights. Some mental health problems could be worry, stress, depression, bipolar disorder, or anxiety. Some physical health problems could be issues such arthritis, back pain, or asthma. Nevertheless, if the culprit behind lost sleep isn't caused currently by stress it will most likely lead to it and when other variables in addition to stress are introduced it can aggravate and worsen any sleep disorder, while also escalating the problem.

There are three stages or levels of sleep disorders that are used to describe sleep patterns that can identify and acknowledge the extent of a sleeping problem. These consist of:

Transient or short term - lasts only a few nights caused from temporary issues.

Intermittent- occurs from time to time over months.

Chronic - occurs every, or the majority of nights lasting over a month.

These different levels of sleeping disorders can be determined as your physician notes your responses to questions they ask referencing your specific sleep problem, such as having trouble falling asleep, staying asleep through the night, or waking early and not being able to fall back to sleep, along with the frequency of these episodes.

Transient or intermittent are usually due to a temporary health or mental problem such as stress. There are a few ways to approach these lesser forms of sleep disorders.

In an attempt to rectify your sleeping problems you will need to:

1. Find and acknowledge the underlying issues that are causing the sleep disorder.

2. Assess and identify any triggers or patterns that worsen your sleeping problems.

3. Experiment with a series of sleep tips to find out what your body needs to give you a restful night's sleep. (list to follow)

The third level, which is *chronic,* will require a minimum of four tasks to help resolve the sleep disorder.

This would be the three issues noted above, plus a very important addition and that is to

4. Seek the help of a physician.

Chronic sleep disorders will more likely result in using a form of medication to get your body back on a healthy path. Your health physician can also help you research the contributing causes to help you get this back under control.

SLEEP TIPS

- Top Recommendation - Stereo pillow speakers to listen to relaxing sounds of nature or music while you drift into sleep.
- Use 'white noise' like the hum of a fan to eliminate some outside noise and create a soothing continuous sound.

- You may apply a concept of thought control to pull the focus of your thoughts in one direction to clear your mind and create focus.
- Use a Sleep Mask to block out any light.
- Shut the television off 30 minutes prior to bedtime and pick up a good book to read.
- Don't lay in bed and worry. It's better to deal with these issues before you go to bed. Accept that if there is nothing you can do about a particular incident right then, you need to be able to set it aside. Think about the positive in any situation.
- Condition your mind to expect sleep, go to bed at night and rise in the morning at the same time every day to maintain the correct balance that your body needs to continue its cycle.
- Use ear plugs to eliminate any unwanted noise.
- Think of words that associate to each letter of the alphabet such as A=apple, B=Banana, C= cat, and so on only visualize these letters and words as you create them. Count backwards from a set number, an easy number is 100 then visualize these numbers as you count them. Visualizing the numbers or letters keeps your mind focused on something trivial until your mind relaxes and drifts off to sleep, rather than planning for the next days activities or worrying over a situation you currently have no control over.
- Eat dinner at a reasonable time so your body has the time to digest the foods before bedtime. If you eat early and are going to experience hunger pangs, have a light snack so that you don't wake in the middle of the night hungry and unable to return to sleep.
- Make use of meditations to relax your body. Place yourself in a serene setting such as by a waterfall surrounded by trees. You are lying at a distance with a small stream passing by as you watch the cascading falls in the background. You hear the water as it falls over the rocks and runs down the mountainside to splash in the water below. Feel the calm breeze in the air. Feel the sun on your body. Smell the trees, plants, and flowers in the air. Continue to hold your vision and relax your body.
- Avoid stimulants in the evening hours including coffee, (especially espresso) tea, soda, alcohol or candy containing high amounts of sugar.
- Don't watch television while lying in bed and only go to bed when you are tired. This allows your body and mind to relate being tired, to bed and to sleep.
- Exercise during the afternoon or early evening but not within the 3 hours prior to bedtime.

- Take a warm bath and put on comfortable clothing to sleep in.
- Make sure you have a comfortable mattress.
- If you or your partner toss and turn a lot though the night, you may what to entertain the idea of investing in a king or queen size bed.
- Keep the temperature comfortable to your benefit at night, depending if you prefer being warm or putting a hint of coolness in the air.
- Don't take naps during the day this may produce alertness in the evening hours when you want to retire for the night.
- Get out of bed if you are not able to fall asleep rather than lay there and fight it, which adds to your own frustrations.
- The last sleep tip is to take advantage of the use of aromatherapy. This can help trigger feelings of relaxation and are available in many fragrances some are noted for having a more calming effect for sleep purposes than others.(More on this in Chapter 8)

If trying these sleep tips does not offer you relief it is best if you consult a professional to rule out any serious health condition.

The last primary need in bringing your bodies health into balance is physical fitness. Physical fitness is the overall result of regular exercise, proper nutrition, and rest. When all of these functions are working in harmony within the body, the body's ability to perform efficiently and effectively in work and leisure activities are at their peek performance. Many physical activities are often practiced to strengthen muscles and the cardiovascular system, as well as to hone athletic skills. When you take into consideration physical fitness, you immediately associate exercise with the release of endorphins that are neurotransmitters. These neurotransmitters reduce pain and anxiety and enhance the immune system.

(Cernsj and Kolster 1999, 26) "Regular physical endurance training leads to a reduction in the heart rate, deeper breathing and an increase in the breaths per minute volume. This means that a sports practitioner exchanges a greater volume of air in his or her lungs than someone who does not practice. In this way the body receives more oxygen. The improved use of breathing means that initially the heart rate of people involved in sport does not increase when they are under stress. The active person deepens his or her breathing and thus does not become so breathless. This in turn has a positive impact on the individual's heart rate and blood pressure."

Exercise can also improve mental health and help prevent depression. Endorphin production is the so-called "runner's high", which is said to occur when strenuous exercise takes a person over a threshold that activates endorphin production. These endorphins are released during long continuous workouts, when the level of intensity is between moderate and high and breathing is difficult.

Exercise is a stress reduction technique no matter what the activity—this will provide you with a means of releasing built-up tension. You may be interested in joining a softball team, or if this is too physically strenuous, taking a brisk walk may be more your style. You might consider visiting a gym or setting up some fitness equipment in the privacy of your own home. If you work out using exercise equipment, you may find it more enjoyable to purchase a small DVD player to watch one of your favorite movies as you work out or use a CD player to listen to music, this will distract you from feeling fatigued, as well as encourage coordination as you keep up with the rhythm of the beat. As long as you are active on a daily basis (or at the very least every other day), you will be providing your body with the physical fitness sustenance needed to create balance within your mind and body.

Make exercise an activity that you enjoy doing and alternate your activities to avoid getting bored. Some fun and entertaining stress reduction exercises are listed below.

- Walking
- Hiking
- Exercise DVD's to dance
- Biking
- Skiing
- Swimming
- Skating (ice or roller)
- Jogging
- Tennis
- Kick boxing
- Aerobics
- Weight lifting
- Water aerobics
- Punching bag (human targets not an option)
- Household chores and working in the yard

It also counts when you vacuum, mop, rake leaves, weed, or shovel snow. Today's working environments are more and more sensing the need of different kinds of physical fitness activity to enhance productivity and reduce job stress. Some of the larger corporations house their own fitness gym for their employees, with the knowledge that physical fitness increases productivity by breaking the repetitiveness and re-energizing your thoughts.

CHAPTER 5
BALANCE RELATIONSHIPS / HOME LIFE

We have a tendency to validate our own sense of worth by the relationships we have with others, how we feel when we are with them and how important or special they make us feel. Family gives us a feeling of warmth, support, and security as does a significant other. When we are single we depend on friends and general acquaintances to give us the companionship that we as human beings rely on. How we view relationships and interact in relationships is an important part of stress reduction. The success of a relationship hinges on positive thinking, rather than judgmental thinking.

In this chapter we will discuss being interactive in a relationship. A large part of this will focus on financial difficulties, since this is a number one stress that can destroy relationships. We will review some ways that we can lessen the impact of these financial stressors. We'll also speculate on options you have to be socially interactive, if you are single. Lastly, you will discover how keeping organized at home can alleviate a lot of stress from your life.

I like the recipe that I made that has to do with what is important in a relationship posted below. Let's face it: It takes two to make a relationship and both have to be willing to work on it for it to become unbreakable.

Recipe for Relationships

Take a lot of love, honesty, loyalty, trust, pride, support, respect, and understanding, have both partners mix these ingredients together, and then add a dash of playfulness and a pinch of humility. Stir well until blended. Once blending is complete, have each partner add two cups of communication to the bowl. Continue to stir for the duration of the relationship.

We all want an enjoyable relationship that contains all of these ingredients, but it's up to both partners as to what ingredients they are willing to add, as well as how they are willing to compromise.

Stress in a relationship becomes more of an issue after the first couple of years. Chances are when you first met your partner (or a past partner if you are currently single) there was some form of immediate attraction, usually but not all the time a physical attraction. This attraction prompted you to pursue this relationship.

Through the first months of your relationship, you continued to find attributes of your partner that you truly admired. You enjoyed being alone to share time with each other. You talked for hours on end without boredom. This person made you relax and made you laugh. Stress in other relationships may have existed but not in this one. You couldn't wait until the day's end, when your separate paths would cross once again.

When the phone rang, and you heard that voice, picturing this person in your mind you felt happy and content. So much of your life seemed right, and the thought of being in this person's arms was a feeling of utopia. This is natural in the beginning of any relationship. You experience such feelings when you explore any new territory in your life. Mystery and Anticipation awaited you.... just like the child whose mind begins as a clear slate you felt overwhelming emotions of excitement, wonder, and curiosity.

Then, as years went by, you may have shifted your focus to things that irritated you about this person. Perhaps this person is a procrastinator or is not as neat or organized as you would like them to be. Stress in the relationship all of a sudden appears as you find yourself making comments that pronounce your frustrations. More time goes by and you find that you've grown to be resentful. You find yourself retaliating in silence, while other times you are defending your positions and beliefs of how you feel things should be done.

What's happening? Your life was once surrounded by joy, laughter, and happiness. How could you have gotten along so well, for so long, with this person and now feel that everything has changed?

Since we all live with stress every day, stress and relationships go hand in hand. You are not the only one harboring these feelings. Don't worry. Everything evolves and changes but mostly in these cases it is your perception that has changed and that can be reversed or at the least altered. At these crossroads in a relationship, we need to place our focus on rekindling those feelings of desire and work on setting those negative feelings on a shelf...a high shelf.

Make some quiet time to reassess your thoughts. Take away for an instant all the negative things you dwell on that concern your partner, wipe them from your thoughts. Then think of the first months that you spent together. Close your eyes, take your time and think of the places that you used to go together and the things that you use to do. Do you remember those feelings of strong attachment that you felt and the yearning you had in your heart just to be in the same proximity of your partner?

It may seem as a surprise to you but these feelings have never left you. You have piled on all of your negative thoughts until you successfully buried the feelings of excitement and wonder. You have unintentionally stunted the growth of your relationship.

You chose your partner as the person you wanted to share your life's experiences with. It's not intended to be all glitter and romance it's meant to be about sharing, growth, and emotional support. We can acknowledge that both partners have their own faults. We are human and this is expected, but you can't let them take over the relationship or they will smoother it.

Use communication and consider some technique to reignite the love you buried inside. The rest will follow. Every relationship needs stimulus to keep it alive. My personal recommendation is to create a romantic atmosphere at home with a fireplace that can be used over and over again. I have had one for at least 9 years and I always know I can create a romantic evening on a whim, pull out some wine, light some candles and set them on the table, then light a fire in the fireplace - instant romance just add water (kidding about the water that's a different recipe but the fireplace works wonders). Save the money from outings and snuggle up together, have dinner, a glass of wine, a little talk and a lot of laughter. Retail outlets offer both, Gel or electric fireplaces if you can't afford the remodel expense to add one to your home. Take the time to do something for you, to bring this enjoyment back into your life.

FINANCIAL BALANCE

The **fifth** key habit to avoid when attempting to reduce stress that may cause us even more stress and cause damage to our health is compulsive spending.

Money/Shopping– When you are stressed you may spend money to make you feel good / Spending money puts you in debt escalating your stress. / So you spend more money.

(Washington Post - Nancy Trejos) "For people already in the throes of addiction, the economy tanking is just another stressor," said Terry Shulman, a Detroit therapist who specializes in addictions. "It's no different than the alcoholic afraid of losing a job or money, but they're still drinking. I think particularly if people feel, 'I'm not going to have a retirement fund, I'm not going to be able to afford the house of my dreams, then I'm going to get nice things, clothing, electronics."

"Even mounting bills aren't enough to keep some hard-core shopaholics from spending money on clothing, vacations or meals at fine restaurants, psychiatrists and financial planners said. In some cases, these experts said, a flailing economy encourages such behavior."

We start this binge on a negative trigger like stress and try to comfort our self by rationalizations saying such statements as, "this makes me feel good," "buying clothes makes me look good and I want to be happy and feel better," but when the bills arrive, we don't have the 'feel better' mindset, it's more like stress. So we return to the same negative thinking within days and the cycle starts over again.

Some of the worst stressors in a relationship have to do with money and finance. Financial security used to mean that you needed only one breadwinner in the family. You could count on the partner at home to have dinner prepared, clean clothes ready to wear, and household duties attended to when you arrived home after a hard day's work.

With the skyrocketing costs of materials and natural resources, coupled with continuous rising health plans and taxes, among other expenses, it has become necessary in most middle income families that both partners earn an income. This has introduced a whole new level of stress within the family, when the household responsibilities need to be shared between both parties. Families will continuously struggle with money issues but the successful relationships will strive to keep the communications open, support one another, and work to keep their relationship strong.

Economical difficulties also come into play with our misplaced values centering on prestige, many individuals tend to judge their life by how many toys they have. People tend to have the "Have to have it all" attitude, and for many this puts them over the edge monetarily causing stress within the family unit to increase to unmanageable levels. Debt seems to have become a normal part of life, but it is far from normal and far from healthy.

To add to this, most live paycheck to paycheck and place additional wants and wishes on a credit card. When they are not able to pay the balance at the end of the month, the interest begins to accumulate. Before they realize their errors, they are paying the credit card company their interest on a monthly basis along with a meager few dollars towards their original purchase. As bills accumulate, so does the financial burden and their stress. With inadequate salaries in comparison to their yearning desires, they find it difficult to meet the monthly payments that have mounted.

It's time to slow down and take stock in what is truly valuable in our lives. Reevaluate your assets and your income and take action to rectify, adjust, and simplify your needs. Become knowledgeable towards money. Realize what money you are giving away as you pay those high interest rates.

If you are currently in debt over your head, before you make a decision that you feel is the best way for you to move forward, research your choices on a particular debt consolidation agency or look into the pro's and con's of filing bankruptcy. It's still your money that you are dealing with, so to avoid piling one mistake on top of the other, gather all the knowledge available to you and don't rush into anything. Try to become familiar with some financial tips that can start saving you money today, while at the same time conduct a financial reassessment on your current assets. Determine further ways to save money and/or dispose of items you can do without. If it costs you more to keep an item, than the benefits or entertainment that the item offers, it may be time to sell it and remove this weight from your shoulders that is dragging you down.

I can't stress this enough... Don't jump from the frying pan into the fire!!! If you speak with someone about financial management or debt consolidation, don't make any immediate decisions. It took you some time to get into this bind, a couple more days won't break the bank no matter what they say... don't rush. Let them know you will need some time to think about this option and you will get back with them in a couple of days.

Financial reassessments will help you gain control over your finances and obligations, reduce your stress, as well as re-address your desires and needs. You may believe you have control over your money, but when you overextend yourself, you lose your control to your finances and to your possessions. Your possessions begin to command your life. The more toys that you have, the less time you may have to actually enjoy them.

These financial tips are small tokens that can reduce your stress while at the same time earn or save you hundreds of dollars or more.

- **Assessing your needs** - Before committing to a substantial purchase, take the time to do a financial reassessment on the item in question. Every possession that you acquire places demands on your time for its continued maintenance, this can increase stress in your life and decrease cash in your pocket.

When securing a loan you not only need to take into consideration the monthly payment obligations. Consider the interest rate that you will be paying and the expenses you will incur for care and upkeep, as well as repairs and maintenance.

Careful consideration, rather than compulsive purchasing, may save you thousands. Learn to monitor your purchases, don't shop impulsively, and most of all, don't overextend yourself or your family by creating debt that becomes more of a hindrance than a pleasure.

- **Clean House** - If you are already overextended, consider alternative options to resolve your issues. Be brutally honest about what you truly need in your life and what you can let go of.

In regards to financial reassessment ask yourself the following questions to help assess your needs:

What items are weighing me down?

What financial obligations am I committed to?

Review the need for each of these items by asking yourself further questions:

Do I get enough use out of the item to warrant the debt in time and money that I contribute to it?

What items can I release that would free up my obligations and give me more time to enjoy what I value most?

- **Consolidation** - If you are struggling to relieve yourself from debt, it is best to consider consolidating your bills into one payment. Check with your local bank or a consolidation company. Remember don't rush into making any immediate decision.

Make purchases using cash whenever possible.

Only keep one credit card for emergency purposes or lump sum purchases (small sums), that you need but don't have the cash on hand to purchase at the time. At the end of the month, be sure that you can pay the balance in full to avoid interest charges. Paying the bill in full keeps you from spending more than your monthly salary.

We unknowingly bind ourselves with stress and drain our own energies by cluttering our lives. Once you have completed these three steps it is important that you do not backslide and recreate bills that you have just gained control over.

Yard Sale - The next step to relieving clutter from your life involves going from room to room throughout your house, including the garage, attic, shed, and basement. Start sweeping the clutter out completing one room at a time and feel the energy being restored in each phase. If the item offers you no benefit, don't hold onto it. This is a time to simplify your life. Be strong and firm; the end results will be well worth your effort. Organize a yard sale and use the profits to your advantage by having a special night out, placing it towards a future vacation, or paying a bill that may be due.

Social Gatherings - Christmas is the best example. If you are having a gathering, don't say, "No" when an individual offers to bring something, have a list of possibilities in your mind and say, "That would be wonderful!" This way you will be able to relax and enjoy the gathering more, while also saving some expense.

Driving - If you spend time on the road, plan your trips so that you are not back tracking and retracing your steps. Gas is money and time is priceless. This is time management, as well as a financial tip. Make up a list and line up your stops. If you drive for a living you may be able to stop to pay a utility bill, cash a check, or stop at the drugstore as you are passing their facility during the week.

Lunch - Rather than spend $5 - $10 dollars on eating out for lunch or picking something up every day, pack your lunch and take it to work with you. This is not only a financial tip but a health tip since you will avoid all of those high fat, fast food places and quick pick me up foods, such as pizza or burgers.

Beating the Jones's - Who cares about the Jones's (If this is your name please do not take this personally), focus on your needs don't try to impress someone who has little to nothing to do with your life. Who cares what they have, they may be struggling just to pay bills and you're both racing each other to see who can get buried in debt the fastest. It may be better if you shared your financial tips with them!

Non-perishables - Items that you will always continue to use such as laundry soap, garbage bags, toilet paper, toothpaste, mouth wash, can vegetables or soup, soda, coffee, spices, condiments such as ketchup, mustard, relish, jar goods such as spaghetti sauces or gravies and many other products, can be purchased when on sale and stocked for future use. Create a space in your garage, basement, or shed, anywhere there is some space you can utilize and place shelves to stock up on these items. This alone can save hundreds for you.

Gifts - Shop for birthdays, anniversaries, Christmas and any other occasions that you traditionally give gifts for over the year, during the periods when retail prices plummet. This would be after the Christmas holiday season, end of winter sales, end of summer sales, just before the school year starts, and on your regular holidays throughout the year, New Years Day sales, Memorial Day sales, and Labor Day sales. Always look for items all year not just one week before the occasion. Your highest cost shopping months are of course, the months of October through December 25th.

Dollar Stores - These are great to purchase occasional cards at two for a dollar. Take the time to stop by and see what they have to offer. You'll be amazed at how the items there, are comparable to what you purchase in department stores at much higher prices.

Redecorating – To save money when you are looking for something new to spruce up the house try rearranging. Take all of your decorative accessories from every room, clean and place them back in different locations. This is a great way to get a fresh new look with zero spending.

Bottom line, learn to be thrifty and stretch your dollar to get more enjoyment out of it. Above all else, take inventory and be thankful for all that you have and all that you have accomplished. Get started with the implementation of your financial tips today to start saving. Don't let financial problems dictate the stress between you and your partner, make it a game of saving money and have fun using your imagination.

Financial strains in a relationship are one of the strongest issues to overcome but there are other requirements that need your commitment, to keep the relationship alive and thriving. To decipher your problems, it's important to act as a team and put your powers of problem solving techniques into action. Whether you have taken vows or not, living together has its commitments. Here are a few tips to reduce other relationship stressors and keep happiness in the forefront.

Communicate – Communication is an important issue when you spend little time crossing paths due to your separate responsibilities. Take an evening to yourselves. Plan on just the two of you taking an evening away together at least once a week. Life is busy, talking for hours as you use to do often gets pushed to the back burner. Make the time to share and create more memories. A walk on the beach or on a nature trail, dinner at a quaint little restaurant, or maybe just going to a favorite spot to watch the sunset. This will give you the alone time without any distractions, where you can simply focus on each other.

Support - Partners are very strong support resources. Once you form a partnership with someone, that person becomes the strongest resource for personal growth. You depend on that person's honesty but most importantly, you depend on his or her faith in you. When someone has faith in you, it serves as a catapult to encourage you to move forward and to remind you of the strengths that you possess but sometimes lose sight of.

Everyone needs encouragement and compliments on a regular basis. You form a team when you decide to share your life with another. Although you usually branch out to follow some separate paths in life that are set in front of you, each day you retreat back to your partner for rejuvenation, love, and of course, support.

Hobbies – It is especially helpful to have a mutual interest in some category of hobby. This could be bowling, jogging, physical fitness where you can work out together at the gym, gardening, or something along the same lines that you both can share together. Continuing to make new memories enforces the bond and strengthens your love. Living together and playing together, means staying together.

If you don't have a mutual interest currently, this is a great conversation piece. What activity can we partake in together? There is a variety of hobbies, you just need to agree on something that you both enjoy and will look forward to doing collectively. (See physical fitness and hobbies under relaxation techniques)

Romance - If you don't feel like going out for an evening, another option may be to make a nice dinner at home. Include candle light and maybe a little wine (alcoholic or non-alcoholic). This will offer the time to focus on each other. Later in the evening after dinner maybe you can plan on popping some popcorn and watching a movie. Sit next to each other and merely enjoy being together.

Children – Spend quality time with the children. If you have children, this can be a very large part of your life together and an important part to share with each other. They have been brought into this world and now look to you to show them the way. Talk to them about challenges that they face and the daily issues they deal with. Give them the emotional support they crave. Be together and present at school functions and activities. Children are a very important part of the future of our planet. They will use the people closest to them as their role models, let this be you.

Both partners are responsible to work at keeping the love and spark of fire alive in any relationship. These are only a few ideas. Take the time to communicate with each other and come up with some of your own. Be happy and enjoy your partner.

If you currently don't have a partner then you know living single has its advantages and has its disadvantages, as does everything else in life. It has been noted several times over the years that married individuals and partners tend to live longer and less stressful lives, than those of single individuals. There are many speculations as to why this occurs. One reason is the fact that your significant other permits you to release stress by being your sounding board, your mediator, and your support system.

If you are single you can develop this same comfort by making close friendships. Religious sects offer relief, as well as other groups that share similar interests as you. Get involved with people through hobbies that you enjoy partaking in. Join a bowling league, or maybe do volunteer work.

Support groups are an excellent option for individuals to use to expand their interaction in the social arena. When you are single you value the reassurance and security that these groups can offer. Support groups have been established worldwide for different reasons, some are interactive with sports or hobbies, some provide phone support when you need someone to talk to, and some provide gatherings where individuals can share their experiences, both the ups and downs. Besides being an outstanding resource of knowledge, they are a strong means of emotional support. It is a well known fact that by reaching out to help another, we inevitably help ourselves.

When first visiting a support group, as with every other initial social interaction, you may feel nervous and awkward. Be sure to take into account that every person there most likely felt nervous and awkward as they made their first approach. If you don't act nervous, you won't be perceived as being nervous. Just keep your focus on being relaxed and friendly. On your first visit, other individuals are going to be excited to have a new face in the group. They'll want to know your name and what lead you to them. After the first two or three visits you'll feel more comfortable. The group itself can become an extended family as you make friends that understand, share, and offer their encouragement.

You may be single but you are never truly alone, many other individuals are in search of new acquaintances. Every warm-blooded being needs companionship, even animals. Living single doesn't have to mean living alone. If you don't mind a little bit of work in exchange for a lot of companionship, a cat that you can confide in is a wonderful outlet. A dog that you can walk, will lead to meeting neighbors that you may have lived next to for years without actually getting acquainted with them. There is no reason that a single person should let social support elude them.

A pet is commonly kept for companionship and enjoyment. The most popular pets are noted for their loyal or playful characteristics, for their attractive appearance, or for their song. The most common house pets are dogs, cats and birds. The bond of a pet and a human grow very strong as they learn to depend on each other to meet their needs. We look at the innocence of a pet as in the innocence of a child. We can depend on the fact that our pet will always be consistent, they will remain excited to see us and they will remain affectionate no matter how we are feeling. For the most part, they have no complicated mix of emotions like we experience.

Pets recognize us as a means of satisfaction for attention and receiving food. We stroke and message the animal, while exchanging body heat for warmth and comfort. They also provide us with health benefits. One of these health benefits is the fact that they can decrease stress that can be caused by loneliness and seclusion. There is now a medically-approved class of therapy pets, mostly dogs, who are brought to visit confined individuals.

Pets have the ability to stimulate us, giving us someone to take care of, someone to exercise with, and someone to help us heal from a physically or psychologically troubled past. In recent years, therapy dogs have been enlisted to help children overcome speech and emotional disorders. Health care professionals have noticed the therapeutic effect of animal companionship, such as lowering blood pressure, and raising spirits, and the demand for therapy dogs continues to grow. There appears to be strong evidence that having a pet can help us lead a longer, healthier life.

Pets learn to sense emotions based on our affection levels and our actions. If we are withdrawn the pet senses that something is wrong or different and attempts to change our behavior maybe by nudging us or curling up to our body for heat when they are unsuccessful at producing a response. A pet can be acquired from a pet store, animal shelter, a breeder, and from private transactions, typically due to the giving away of extra newborns after the birth of a litter.

There are other things you can do in your home to help reduce the stress, besides having a pet. This last topic that we are discussing in this chapter to bring balance into our relationships and home life is the topic of organization.

Organization is an invisible source of stress that may be the most frequently looked over cause of stress in many cases. Organization is also one of the most frequent stressors we place upon ourselves, that can be easily rectified. Possibly because we think it takes to much time to put things in proper order, but think of how many times you have spent 10 minutes, 30 minutes, maybe an hour, trying to locate something you know that you set right there on the counter, or put right there in the drawer. When you go to retrieve it suddenly it has disappeared, it's not where you thought you had put it. When you take the time to put things in order, it keeps everything you need at your finger tips.

Considering that we only have twenty-four hours in a day, it's imperative that we find corners to cut. If you break down your twenty-four hours, they may look something like this:

8 hours sleep
1 hour shower, groom, and dress
8 hours work
1.5 hours commute to and from work (or total drive time)
2.5 hours preparing, eating, and cleaning up after 3 meals

This = 3 Hours of Free Time.

These are only the necessities, but they add up to a whopping twenty-one hours. This in a nutshell, is why keeping both your home life and your work life in order are so important. You always have basic rules to follow.

Rule #1 List
Rule #2 Lists
Rule #3 More Lists

Do you need to ask why? For two reasons; we need to be able to see all of our tasks so that we can put them in priority order and also, by placing your thoughts on paper, this will ensure that you won't accidentally neglect any tasks or worse, totally forget about something. The rules are easy to memorize and keep in order.

Take a few minutes of your day and jot down your to-do's on a piece of paper. To begin to identify your priorities you will need to determine what tasks will need your immediate attention and move those to the top of the list, or number them on the paper. Now choose your top priority, place the remainder of the items on the lists to the side and focus 100 percent of your thoughts on each task in due order. You have now reduced the stress you felt from being overwhelmed with to much clutter in your mind.

No, it isn't always that uncomplicated. You may have other issues come into play throughout the day, so you will have to go back to basics, you will either have to juggle to place something on your priority list to complete today, place it on a list to be done tomorrow, or delegate it to another party to complete but don't forget to follow-up to be sure it gets completed.

Your list will be never ending—what may not get done today will move to tomorrow; what isn't done tomorrow should move to the next day's list, and so on. As long as a task is in the process of completion, you won't forget it. Once you have completed the task in full, then and only then, should you remove it from the list.

Rule #4

Remove the material clutter from your life!! As stated earlier, simplifying your space is the process of organizing your belongings and letting go of the excess, until your surroundings are peaceful and in order. Once your personal space is cleared, you will be absolutely amazed at the renewed energy and inspiration this generates. If your surroundings are in order and uncluttered your mind will be relaxed, and uncluttered. When your mind is relaxed, your body will follow suit. Remaining relaxed allows you to keep more control over how you react to any given situation that may arise, even a stressful one. You will diffuse daily pressures by establishing and maintaining a mindset of harmony and balance.

We find there seems to never be enough hours in the day to complete everything we would like to do. We rush from the time we get up in the morning until the time that we go to bed. These simple home organization tips will help to generate more desperately needed time. You will discover that by minor alterations, you will feel more relaxed and prepared to face all of your daily activities with ease.

Remember the basics - There is a place for everything and everything in its place. Train yourself and others in your household to put things back where they got them from. If each person becomes responsible for himself in this area, all the cleanup work won't be dumped onto one person. Family members and roommates need to have consideration for others under the same roof. We all have a lack of time and an abundance of stress.

Cooking - If you are the cook within your household and you also work a forty-hour week, there are a few home organization tips that you can use to create more free time in your schedule.

Before you go grocery shopping, organize and plan your meals for the week then shop accordingly. When you prepare a meal, make enough for one or two more additional meals and then freeze the remainders to pull out as an entrée next week.

There are also some great meals in the frozen food section of your supermarket that contain meat, starch, and vegetables all in one bag. There are varieties of chicken, steak, pot roast or pasta. These are wonderful to use if you should forget to pull something from the freezer or you didn't have enough time to prepare as many meals as you needed for the week. Throw in a tossed salad and presto, the meal is complete in minutes with little mess.

If you have a partner, pick one day of the week that he or she agrees to prepare the meal, even if it means picking up a pre-cooked meal at the supermarket on the way home. You may also consider designating one night "delivery night," where you call to order in Chinese or subs and a salad. Be sure to keep healthy in mind when picking up something ready to eat or using a delivery service.

Take turns when it comes to cleaning up after dinner and doing the dishes, or designate separate responsibilities so that each person can chip in and help.

Preparing yourself for the week –When doing the laundry, arrange your closet according to what you are going to wear in the upcoming week. Designate a section of your closet to hang what you have selected and always pick one extra set of clothes in case your mood changes and you don't like what you had picked out for that particular day. This is helpful if you work outside the home to save time and frustration in the mornings, as well as becoming prepared for any unforeseen problems that rob you of precious morning time when you are on a schedule.

Don't forget to select any accessories, such as jewelry and place these to the side, as well as your belts, nylons or socks, and shoes.

Preparing the children for the week – If you are responsible for getting children ready in the morning, apply the same concept by laying five days' of school clothes aside and one back-up outfit. Don't forget the socks or any other essentials.

On school nights, have an assigned space, like a chair, counter, or table, where your children can set their books, book bags, or any other items they are going to take with them the next morning. These tips will not only give you more time in the mornings but also ensure that your day starts out smooth and stress free.

Procrastination is a form of avoiding organization so this needs to be eliminated from your life. Have you ever felt that you are constantly dealing with unpleasant tasks that need to be completed? When dealing with procrastination we can sometimes make life harder on ourselves without even realizing what we are doing.

Maybe it's not so much that you are overloaded with unpleasant tasks every day, as it is that you keep playing this same task over and over in your head day after day and yet again, you ultimately will play tug-a-war in your mind until you convince yourself to put it off until tomorrow. Does that tomorrow ever come? It will come and when it does you will grit your teeth, dig in and complete the task that you have been so much dreading for the last days, weeks or maybe months. Now that the task is done you sit back feeling pretty proud of yourself, glad that it is finally over and ready to go celebrate your accomplishment.

Little did you know that you spent many unnecessary days hurting your own physical and mental well being by dealing with your negative emotions, thoughts and procrastination, which is one of our strongest enemies. This will hamper our ability to complete projects and meet deadlines. This will inject negative emotions that will deplete our energy, obstruct our goals, and shackle us like a ball and chain until it gets what it wants.

What do you do when you have to complete a task that you dread doing? You place this at the end of your task list.

~~~~~ Why? ~~~~~

You spend way more time trying to avoid the task and dreading the task than if you were to place it at the top of your list, get it out of the way, release yourself from this stress, and forget about it, so roll up your sleeves and knock it out of the way.

If you find that you cannot make this task a high priority, then place it on your list of to-do's in its perspective order of importance. Be sure when you get to that item on the list that you don't skip over it. When all is said and done those not so pleasant tasks will still be there...................... waiting for you.

If you choose to not deal with an issue then you give up your right of control over the issue and it will select the path of least resistance.

CHAPTER 6
OCCUPATIONAL STRESS

Occupational stress does not just appear in fast pace jobs, it affects the entire workforce encompassing all types of employment. Work stress can be caused by a variety of factors from poor management, stress directly related to the worker, and other stressors pertaining more to the work environment and conditions. Becoming more aware of what may be causing your stress, will allow you the opportunity to take steps necessary to remedy these issues.

You may be working for a company, that due to lack of training or knowledge, is poorly managed. This is the most difficult to rectify without organizational change. Since you have no control over any of the issues at this level of management, you may try to make accommodations and recommendations in reference to your duties that can reduce your individual stressors. It is a useless battle to try to expand any further than this and may best be rectified by looking for further employment.

A stable and employee oriented company has programs in place for employee support, such as members assistance programs and stress management programs, that teach relaxation techniques, whether it is a class on stress prevention or in house training and positive reinforcement.

Some worker issues may be personality clashes that cause employee conflicts, the speed of interpreting new information when adapting to new job skills, the need for employees to be recognized for a job well done, the inability to expand work knowledge and duties, the inability to take part in decisions that effect your job responsibilities, or even personal problems that stem from outside of work but are additional stressors that are being placed on the worker.

Environmental factors may include issues such as having inadequate equipment to complete the tasks efficiently, having ergonomically incorrect designs for employee comfort and productivity, dealing with an excessive workload with high expectations, even having bad lighting can cause stress and eye fatigue. Physical effects of stress such as fatigue caused by sleep disorders, can escalate to injuries on the job and increase expense to workers compensation claims.

*The **sixth** key habit to avoid when attempting to reduce stress that may cause us even more stress and cause damage to our health is what we choose to do when we take a break from stress at work.*

***Caffeine & Nicotine** - Many individuals get overly stressed at work and have to remove themselves to take a break from their activities. If you do this and reach for a cigarette or a cup of coffee to relax this can have the reverse effects from what you want to experience.*

You may believe that lighting up that cigarette helps you to reduce stress but it is just the opposite. When you return to your work, your body soon starts to reactivate the tensions of nicotine withdrawal. With nicotine dependency you are on a regular rotation with stress build up, once you satisfy the urge the rotation starts anew. Smoking not only causes effects of stress on the body but also the mind. If you are a smoker you know that once the urge starts to rebuild the stronger it gets, the more the thoughts are directed solely on gratification. If you are in a situation where you can't satisfy that urge right away the stress in your mind builds until you feel you are going to burst if you can't satisfy the urge quickly.

Reaching for that coffee (caffeine) or even a soda when you are feeling stressed is also a mistake. Drinking coffee can cause havoc with blood pressure as it slows the blood flow to the brain and can raise your blood pressure. If you already have high blood pressure, then most likely your physician has already recommended that you limit your caffeine intake. Caffeine also interferes with sleep, so if you are increasing your intake of coffee when you are stressed you are pushing yourself to develop another disorder to increase your levels of stress. Every work position from facts and figures to assembly work needs to be alert and functional in his position so blood flow to the brain is important for memory and comprehension, both of which are needed to perform accurately and safely.

Learning and applying time management skills will be effective at work as well as in all other areas of your life. If you haven't already, it would be highly beneficial to take a time management class. If this is not offered by your employer you can usually find these classes at a local college. Other forms of occupational stress that we will look at are listed below.

Causes of Occupational Stress

- Lack of enthusiasm
- Difficult people

- Lack of control
- Monitor your workload
- Bad communication
- Job satisfaction
- Lack of Planning
- Accepting a new job
- Child care
- Queen Bee syndrome
- Breaking habits of a perfectionist

When occupational stress reaches overload you may be showing signs of job burnout. If you detect these symptoms, it is best to act quickly to prevent this from occurring.

Lack of enthusiasm - After years at the same job the lack of variety and boredom may play a part in making you discontent at your place of employment. If the job is monotonous and you feel you could contribute to performing other duties, speak with the supervisor about taking on more or different responsibilities. This may even open up the door for you in further job advancement.

Get together with your co-workers and generate some excitement, there may be some others that are as discontent as you or may just enjoy some variety and fun at work but don't know what to do about it. Creating some friendly competition between co-workers can produce some excitement, develop some contests in your work environment which pertains to the work that you do. Schedule a pot luck lunch day where everyone brings in something to eat. Designate Fridays as ice cream social days and collect money from each employee then select one to go to the store and obtain ice cream and cones. This is really inexpensive maybe fifty cents a person and is something to look forward to.

If your lack of enthusiasm is due to the fact that you want to accomplish more or obtain a career in a different area of specialty, then sign up and attend a night class at your local community college. This gives you something to look forward to as well as building on your future.

Difficult people – Work stress is increased when confronted with a difficult co-worker and finding the underlying source of the problem will be the key to turning around a bad attitude. You will work with many different personalities, some individuals are very sensitive, some are insecure which can cause jealousy, some may be having personal issues, some just flat may not be happy at all.

Let's face it not everyone is going to like you one hundred percent of the time and that's okay. We all have different personalities and sometimes they clash together when you view things from opposite extremes. Give the co-worker the benefit of the doubt. Maybe it isn't you but that they are having personal problems. Be concerned and see if you may be able to help. If they take the opportunity to speak with you, don't discount their feelings, listen to their words and stay on the subject of them don't say, "Yea, once that happened to me and….." Whatever they are feeling may not be rational to you but this is what they are *feeling* not you.

If you are a new employee or have just taken on new responsibilities and you meet up with someone who shows you a lack of favoritism, it may be possible that it is more of a jealousy issue with the co-worker. Be the first to make the approach and ask if it was something you said that made them upset with you.

Place a little tidbit of happiness at their workstation when they are not looking. You can use a piece of candy, a picture, a new pen, or whatever you can think of to cheer their day. Sometimes they are thankful to know that you or anyone for that matter cares enough to take the time to make them smile.

Lack of control – Responsibility without any control may become stressful. If you want to have your words heard in your company, get actively involved and knowledgeable about the entire company, not just your responsibilities. Look at the big picture this will open your mind to making suggestions that will benefit the company not just make your job easier.

Before making a suggestion, review the positive and negative effects of what you are asking for then gather the data to support your suggestion. If you are asking for a new copier and are not successful at obtaining one, consider such things as the companies budget may not be strong enough to handle the purchase. Come up with options if this is the case, what about renting one, then call around and get some prices. Whatever the suggestion get personally involved and active to come up with a resolution, before making the approach to you supervisor. Above all be realistic.

Monitor your workload – Make use of a daily planner. Technology is advancing at a rapid pace and while technology can be beneficial, the consequences can create more stress in our lives. With the increasing amount of resources and much faster means of communications, employees are expected to be able to take on heavier work loads with additional responsibilities but this is to be accomplished in the same forty hour workweek.

If you become over inundated with projects to complete and begin to feel frustrated, take a deep breath and remember that you are not a super person who can leap buildings in a single bound, ask for help. If there is nobody that can help and your supervisor has unrealistic deadlines and expectations, then it is best to let them know what you are up against and see if they can assign someone to help you. Don't take it all on yourself, sometimes your supervisor can unintentionally give you more projects without thinking of what you are already working to complete. If you don't handle the situation, it will bring on an abundance of stress that will cause you to become irritable and temperamental. This will only give you a negative image and hinder completing the work on any project.

It will never be beneficial for you to take the whole world on your shoulders. It's better to focus on completing one project accurately, than three or four projects that are turned in halfheartedly that require more time to review, check mistakes and collect more data. Your supervisor understands this and would prefer the above standard work rather than substandard.

Bad communication - Communication with your superiors is essential to reduce work stress. There are many personalities in this world and each personality possesses positives and negatives as does everything else. If you are having difficulty communicating with your supervisor keep neutral and demonstrate your knowledge, capabilities, and skills that you bring to your position. Do the best you can and know that everything will fall into place with time.

If your boss cannot approach you on your level of communication, then it becomes hard to keep things running smoothly and will increase the amount of work stress that you will experience. This is a form of inadequate leadership. You must always strive to meet on middle ground and most importantly, never give up but try to get closer so that you can better understand that persons work philosophy.

One hand needs to know what the other hand is doing. If you are in charge of one project and then you find that someone else is popping in here and there and making decisions that alter the flow, either politely let that individual know that interferences will only complicate and confuse matters, or back away and let another take over the project if that seems to be the goal that they want to meet. You can simply accept their help and move onto the next project but don't be snippy about it, let them know if they have any questions you will be glad to point them in the right direction.

Job satisfaction - If you wake up in the morning and dread the thought of getting in that vehicle, driving to work, and entering those doors, then you are definitely not satisfied with your job and this will highly increase the amount of stress that you face on a daily basis. That doesn't necessarily mean you need to quit and move on, maybe you just need more of a challenge to keep your interest peaked, or maybe you are so overloaded with work that the stress has become unmanageable.

Whatever the reason is, there are solutions waiting to be found. Take some time and jot down some notes. What do you like about your job and what do you not like about your job. Pinpoint what is making you unhappy and is the cause of your work stress. Once you find that reason, write down all the possible solutions to change this situation, even if you think it is unreasonable or impossible.

After you have ideas in writing, place them to the side for a few days as you mull over your thoughts. You may end up taking partial solutions from a couple of your ideas and find that putting them together is a reasonable solution. Maybe you need to speak to your supervisor and let them know the changes that you are thinking of and ask them if they would be willing to offer some additional suggestions. If you ever approach a supervisor with a problem to discuss always be prepared to offer possible solutions.

There is an answer which is an acceptable solution to all problems but you will need to be the one to initiate a change and take control over the amount of work stress that you experience.

Lack of Planning – Improper planning and implementation of any change causes stress to everyone involved. When given any project or change to apply, be sure you first review the stages of the change with at least one person that the change will directly affect. The reason for this is to take into consideration all of the questions that are posed to see if additional changes, explanations or directions need to be added prior to the final implementation.

Accepting a new job - Entering a new position is a stressful process. You are learning many new procedures to comply with the requirements of the job and its responsibilities, these may feel overwhelming. With time, as with any job, once you learn one procedure and move onto the next your list of challenges keeps decreasing with your knowledge and your comfort level will begin to increase.

Your objective is to keep positive, understand from the beginning that you are accepting new challenges that will help you expand your career. Everyone has to go through an adjustment period both you and the individuals that you will be working with. Be humble and don't be afraid to ask for help, people will respect the fact that you don't come across as a know-it-all. You are also adjusting to a new environment and this will take a week or two before you feel you are walking on solid ground. Remaining positive and displaying a good attitude, will also generate admiration and help gain approval.

Child care - One of the strongest challenges for mothers in the workforce are daycare facilities. This has become a more notable problem over the years as the female workforce has magnified by large numbers. Some larger corporations and governmental agencies have attempted to reduce this work stress by the establishment of in house daycare facilities. This not only reduces the stress placed on the mother but reduces the absenteeism rate that is caused by disruptions in child care resources.

Be sure to visit a daycare facility, meet the employees and take a tour with your child to see how they react to the environment before placing them in this setting. They will also be more comfortable to meet other people with you by their side. Check with the better business bureau and maybe speak to other parents, to see if they have dealt with any problems that you should be aware of before placing your child in the hands of others.

Queen Bee syndrome – Some individual's feel they need to be the center of attention. The queen bee flits and flutters picking up tidbits of honey from others, and then insinuates that without their input the project may have been less than satisfactory. They also tend to collect gossip and disburse it where they feel it may benefit their needs, some may actually thrive on this chaos and it keeps the excitement churning in their life simply for entertainment. Queen Bee's only have moments of gratification, whereas the work oriented individual carries accomplishments forward and builds on experience and success. For the protection of your own image, it's best not to get to friendly with these individuals for more than one reason. You don't want to get involved with rumors and gossip and you don't want to develop a negative image of yourself, especially if your intentions are to someday seek a promotion or letter of recommendation.

Breaking habits of a perfectionist - People who practice this behavior might be subjecting themselves to an even higher level of health risks. Problems occur when the stress response fails to reverse itself and, therefore, does not reset properly. The perfectionist, who oversees the production of other workers, tends to have a high level of stress, most of it due to frustration.

The perfectionist sets high expectations for themselves and no matter how hard they try, or how well they do they never feel as though they can attain their goal or measure up to their own expectations. They will set high expectations not only for themselves but also for those around them. The mere fact that they cannot make the people that surround them work as hard or as efficient as themselves, provokes stressful episodes.

If you are living a life of a perfectionist and don't accept that there will be moments of failure, you are setting yourself up for a devastating blow of reality. (Bradshaw, 1988, [a] 164-165) "Hindsight is what you see so clearly later on. The key word is "later". It is the later interpretation that turns the action into a mistake. A mistake is a label you apply in retrospect. Mistakes are the result of a later interpretation. Hence, mistakes have nothing to do with self-esteem. If you label yourself "bad" because it was a mistake in light of later awareness, you end up punishing yourself for actions you couldn't help performing. Better labels for your past mistakes would be "unwise", "ineffectual" or "fruitless. These terms are a more accurate assessment of your judgment. At the time you always choose the action that seems most likely to meet your needs. The benefits seem at the time to outweigh the disadvantages. The action in any given moment depends on our awareness." We learn from failures, ours as well as others'. The consequences of failure, will only inject more stress into your life if you cannot accept the lessons they offer and move forward with a positive, rather than self-condemning attitude.

To be more effective at work be sure you set realistic goals and deadlines. Remind yourself that there is no such thing as being perfect, and don't place those expectations on anyone else within your work unit. Use task lists to prioritize. Acknowledge to yourself that these tasks may not all get done in one day and that the less important tasks at the bottom of the list may get transferred to tomorrow's list.

Ways to relax and reduce stress at Work

- Listening to music
- Pick and choose your battles
- Learn to say No
- Exercise and keeping fit
- Keeping yourself healthy
- Good nutrition picks

- Laughter
- Meditation

Listening to Music - Music is a contributor to work productivity and positive mood enhancement. Using low background music will create a relaxed atmosphere and in turn, relaxes the employees so they are better equipped to remain calm in a stressful situation. With focus placed on the sounds and songs, there is also less of a chance that interaction in conversation will lead to negative gossip.

Pick and choose your battles - By choosing not to fight any battle you are immediately reducing job stress to '0' in this area.

If you think the battle is worth the fight, then before you say anything to your superiors or co-worker, you need to get prepared. The worst move you can make is to voice an objection, when you haven't got anything other than your objection to back it up. This is called whining. Gather all your facts and figures and organize your thoughts as to what points you want to get across. Always have alternative solutions to any problem that could be taken into consideration.

Learn to say No - It's hard to say "No" and not feel guilty but some people can take advantage of this weakness.

Commitment and loyalty used to be a big part of one's career in the past. Yet today, as a matter of survival, individuals have to put into practice the word "no." If you are involved with a management group that is driven to accomplish more, make more money and become more powerful by using you to dedicate long hours of overtime, then it is most likely that they do not comprehend the values of home, family, and free time. If you are not a workaholic and have other interests in your life, you may need to find an organization that has or respects these same values.

Your family and the time you spend with them are not replaceable. To accomplish goals you need to be able to do your job well and complete your assignments, but to place balance and stability in your life, it is definitely not advisable for your health and for your family to consume yourself with these obligations and tasks.

If your co-workers are always asking for help or favors so they can accomplish their own tasks, be up front and honest with them if they are getting out of hand. Let them know you don't mind helping once in a while but you have your own responsibilities also.

Exercise and Keeping Fit – Keep a pair of walking shoes stashed at work—under your desk, in your locker, or wherever is easiest to get to so that you can slip them on and take a nice brisk walk. At break or at lunch you can walk around the building or around the block. It's great if you have stairs, since they provide an alternative in extreme weather conditions. Any form of physical activity will provide you with renewed strength and energy for the days remaining tasks.

Keeping Yourself Healthy - You may have good intentions as you slave to prove yourself as a multi-task individual. You may work long hours to show devotion and loyalty to your profession. But by always thinking of everyone else, you miss the signals of the needs that your mind and body are giving you. It is important to remember that you always need to schedule time for yourself and keep it just as you would a doctor's appointment. Your mental health and physical health will be strong determining factors as to whether you are successful or not. Working non-stop you may think is good for your career and family, but the stress placed on yourself affects every part of your life. Be sure to take a lunch break, leave work on time, and enjoy your days off and relax. Spend your free time doing something that brings joy into your life.

Good Nutrition Picks – Rather than bringing in donuts, cupcakes, cookies, cakes and such, agree as a group to try to focus more on nutrition when bringing in a treat for the office. Choose muffins, bagels, strawberries, apples, oranges, grapes. Any item that holds less fat, less sugar, and more fiber and vitamins will promote health and wellness along with giving you a more positive outlook during the day.

High fat and sugar will drain your energy and you will feel as if you are dragging through the day to reach the end of your shift. If you go out for lunch, try to reduce your intake of fat as well as your portion size. Don't go to an open buffet, over eat and then return to work tired and uncomfortable.

Laughter - Laughter releases morphine-like *endorphins*, which are secreted by the pituitary gland. This substance is a stress reducing hormone that controls pain and pleasure. A good laugh actually counteracts stress and its affects on your health. If you take breaks during the day, having around a comical book to read or CD to listen to is helpful as a method of stress reduction. Be sure to keep it clean and not offensive if anyone other than you will have access to these items. Having fun at work is an important part of enjoying your job.

Meditation – Take some time within your day to sit back, close your eyes and complete the quick fix meditation. This only takes minutes which is why it is very helpful in a work setting. You will find the directions for this exercise under relaxation techniques found in Chapter 8.

Environmental Factors – If you are dealing with any form of environmental problems it is to your own best interest to bring these to the attention of your supervisor. This may range from proper seating, lighting, air quality, or a number of other things. Chances are that your supervisor is not even aware of the problem so until it is brought to their attention it will not be corrected.

There is not any work environment that is stress-free. So, what is the difference between stress and burnout? Stress is caused when individuals are very involved in their job and while stressful situations will come into play, they can be swiftly resolved with limited adjustments. Individuals that care about their position and strive to provide high-quality work deal with the stress of having high self expectations and this prompts motivation and drive to accomplish tasks and to continue to push forward to meet goals but when things go wrong, stress can lead to burnout.

Stress leads to burnout if the stress is continuous (chronic) and the stressors are not being resolved or eliminated in the working environment. This causes feelings of helplessness and despair which consequently leads to a loss of interest along with motivation. This contributes to poor performance, high absenteeism, high turnover rate, and costs focused on health issues. This has a negative influence on the business, as well as the employee. Additionally, job burnout is more prevalent if you are continuously working in a repetitive manner day after day without the variety of change, an example of this would be an assembly line job. Job satisfaction becomes excessively frustrating and you become mentally, physically, and emotionally drained.

(Ross, 2002, 83) "Pressures in the workplace have skyrocketed. There's been a 700 percent increase in workmen's comp claims for mental stress claims since the 1980's in California alone, and 25-40 percent of workers nationally now report stress burnout, particularly women with children. Stress ranks second only to family crisis among problems in the workplace."

Women may have a higher risk of job burnout simply because of the multiple roles they hold in society. They may perceive that they need to do-it-all as a mother, a wife, a caregiver, and career women. In an effort to do-it-all they spread themselves to thin and after an extended amount of time, they unintentionally find they have worked themselves straight into burnout.

Many other sources can also be contributed to burnout. If you are experiencing trouble in any of the areas listed below, pull your focus in this direction and work to resolve these situations. If the situations are out of your control, then bring this to the attention of your supervisor for rectification.

Heightened pressure for productivity
Improper or poor training
Challenges become overpowering with unreasonable demands
Unorganized surroundings
Poorly thought out implementation of changes
Doubling workload in absence of proper staffing
Little communication which limits the growth of stimulation that can
lead to expressive ideas and suffocates creative thinking
Overextended hours
Bureaucratic red tape
Low salary in comparison to job duties and responsibilities
Poor chances for advancement
Negative office politics and disputes among staff members
Quarreling and tension in the workplace

If problems persist you may want to research another job field. There is no reason why you should be expected to work in an atmosphere of disarray. It is crucial to be happy in your work life since a large quantity of time is spent at your place of employment. If you are not happy at work, you will bring these emotions home with you and this will result in even more dysfunction.

What about organization at work? Yes, it's the same as organization at home. You will be more effective and efficient. Your mind will be more clear and able to handle multiple tasks with less stress. Below are some tips that may help you in this area.

Color Code Folders – Use color coded files to dedicate to each given topic and then each of the sub categories of that topic. For instance let's say that I am a buyer for a small department store. I would separate the store into pieces of categories such as Kitchen, Garden, Hardware, Toys, etc. and then I take one category using red folders, lets use kitchen, and break that down placing sub-categories of kitchen behind the main folder like, pots, mixing bowls, silverware, etc. all using red folders. Then use a different color for the next category and its sub-categories and so on. In your main folder you may choose to keep material like different vendor solicitations or lists of what that department should stock. In its sub-categories, such as pots, you may have a list of each vendor you purchase from – the item – the description - how many you should stock – wholesale price – and retail price of each piece. You will be able to find any file quickly and efficiently.

Junk Drawer – Simple rule…If its junk throw it away. If it is something you plan to keep at work find an appropriate place to put it. Use a folder, plastic bin, post it on a bulletin board or place it into a marked container.

Calendars – Make use of a wall calendar and a desk calendar and separate their uses for assigned topics so that at a quick glance you have the information that you need.

Organizers – Organizers also have calendars to track important dates and meetings, but you should also keep ongoing lists of questions you need to ask. Using the same department store adventure lets say I have some questions for a vendor in reference to his product, or maybe I am contemplating adding another line of items. Rather than calling the vendor each time I thought of a question, I would just jot the question in my organizer.

When the vender and I spoke next, I could open my organizer to reference all of the questions that I had listed to ask and I would note key words next to the question that makes it easier to retrieve from memory what the response to the question was.

Phone numbers – File phone numbers by how you most easily know your contacts. Traditionally we are taught to file all correspondence numbers by their last name but it is far easier to remember a first name than it is a last. It may be easier to file by first name, or by company name.

Organize your office - By focusing on work organization you should seldom have piles of paperwork and unfinished projects (unless they are organized piles and projects). Not everything can be done right away—we have accepted this bit of knowledge.

When you receive an important directive or information that you may need to refer to at a later date, either file it or act on it but don't make piles of papers that in a week will take you hours to go through, re-read, and file in their appropriate files, this is doubling your work and stealing time that you could be using for something more important. By operating more efficiently and smoothly, you will reduce your frustration, save yourself time and therefore, reduce the stress you place on yourself.

Computer and e-mail – Just as the color coded files, you will make one folder for your category, open that folder and then create all of your sub-categories that are placed into that folder. Your computer files are just as your file cabinet folders accept these are condensed in a much smaller space.

Always back up the hard drive of your computer to protect from any viruses that may contaminate your files forcing you to have to dump everything on your computer.

Make Use of Cabinets and Containers - If your place of employment has you dealing with paperwork, it is essential to keep this organized for easy retrieval. There is an enormous amount of organizational tools to help you, from bins, boxes, containers, files, and way too many more varieties to list here, utilize them.

When you receive a call in relation to a question, you want to be able to easily reference material to find an answer. You will become more efficient in your abilities to do your job and increase your skills which will be noticed and may lead you to advancing in your career.

Organizing your thoughts – Work organization isn't all about paper. When you are presented with a frustrating problem, train yourself not to react immediately but to gather and organize your thoughts and information, then get back to the person at a later time. Never rely on your immediate response, since when you are frustrated you tend to act and think in an irrational manner. Take the time to back away from the situation and think about how you want to respond then deal with the issue when you are ready to do so.

Create the Atmosphere - Be certain that you create an atmosphere not only of relaxation but of work organization and professionalism.

Take inventory of the atmosphere that surrounds you at work. If you work in a position that allows you to inject some personality into your workspace do so, but keep certain priorities in mind. If you can choose paint or wallpaper for your immediate surroundings, lean towards the soft colors, which will give you a feeling of peace.

When you choose decorative pieces to place in your space, take your time with these selections. Choose items that: bring back good memories, things that make you smile, candles or potpourri to provide some added atmosphere as well as a soothing scent in the air, and if you don't already have one, you may want to purchase a simple CD player and some CD's with relaxing sounds to keep you focused on calming thoughts.

Learn to delegate - Sometimes individuals don't want to delegate simply because they want to prove to someone that they are capable and responsible to complete many tasks. Some may not want to teach or help another individual learn and advance, fearing they are placing their own position in jeopardy. Perfectionists feel that they are the only ones able to complete the task accurately, and they find it difficult to place faith in others.

Delegating contributes to your work organization, while someone may not undertake the task the same way as you, delegating will create a much-needed gap in your schedule for you to organize or take that needed break that re-energizes you, or to save time and start the next project. You will still need to follow up on the work you have delegated to be sure it is complete and accurate, but this takes much less time than completing the project yourself. By letting go of some control, you are giving someone else the opportunity to learn.

It is best to create a balance with fun, humor, and compassion with your co-workers and intermingle this with your enthusiasm of strong work ethics to gain respect and guide others to mimic your enthusiasm. Keeping a positive attitude above everything is a strong goal to strive towards. Our personalities create our world. It explains how we become optimistic or pessimistic. It shapes our goals, our attitude toward work, relationships, and how we raise our children, ultimately predicting whether or not we will fulfill our potential. If you work on a positive attitude on a daily basis you will find stress eventually will not be able to penetrate your shield of optimism and will encourage others to follow suit.

CHAPTER 7
PERCEPTION AND POSITIVE THINKING

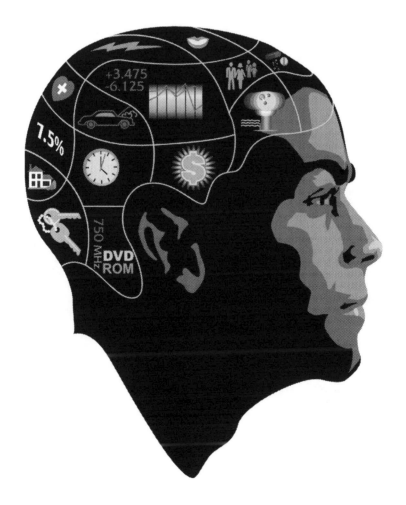

*"Adopting the right attitude
can convert a negative stress
into a positive one."
Hans Selye*

Perception is your interpretation of events through your observations and thought process. Your perception is not necessarily reality, as we discovered in the example given in chapter 1 describing acute stress. Your anger caused negative responses and you perceived that the individual in the vehicle in front of you was the cause of you almost becoming involved in an accident.

What is positive thinking? Let me take the round about way in explaining this. We are made up of flesh, bones, muscles, ligaments etc., but what makes us tick? What gives us the desire to get up in the morning? Our bodies are shells that can transport us from one location to another as well as allow us to interact with the world by our movements, we use our legs and spine to walk, our arms to reach or our fingers to grasp items. We are nothing without our brains that give us the ability of imagination with our minds. Thoughts are what create you as an individual. What make us different in comparison to others besides our visual appearance are our thought patterns and the way that we perceive events as they occur in our lives. These things mold our world.

Positive thinking is a form of thought that accompanies only good emotions, intentions and perceptions. A person that thinks positive will display qualities such as being patient, not taking things personally, not holding grudges, etc. by using accumulated knowledge, values, and logical thinking to decipher actions. They are relaxed and emit positive energy, which is noticeable in their interactions using facial expressions, tone of voice, and physical movements. They are encouraging and give confidence to others, as well as being cheerful and confident in their demeanor. They have an optimistic attitude and anticipate that only good things will happen today. If they experience an inconvenience or frustrating occurrence they are constructive in resolving the issue if it can be changed, if it cannot be changed they look at the positive aspects and accept the situation as it is. By living with this mentality they experience inner peace. They are not at odds with the world and struggling to make a square peg fit into a round hole.

Your thoughts determine how you perceive something at any given time. Today you may be in a really uplifting and carefree mood with a positive attitude. A stressful situation occurs and you perceive this as a small obstacle in the road and handle the situation swiftly and successfully. Tomorrow you are extremely tired since you had a disagreement with your spouse and spent most of the night tossing and turning. There was no coffee this morning and you are carrying a negative attitude. The identical stressful situation occurs, you throw your hands in the air and grumble how it seems nothing can go right and everyone always expects you to fix everything. Two identical situations, but one applies a positive attitude and one applies a negative.

We tend to move blindly through life and let others dictate how we feel, how we act and even how we treat others. We let other people control our lives as well as the possessions that we choose to own as discussed in chapter five with our financial burdens and reckless spending. To resolve these issues and take back the control of our lives we must look within and decide what we feel is important, what will grant us peace and bring balance back to our lives. We need the happiness that is buried inside, covered with worry, fear and many negative thoughts.

Many times we search, yet we don't know what we are looking for. We set goals and then work feverishly to attain them, but this is never good enough so we set higher goals. The goals we set seem to be what we want at the time that we set them, but once there it doesn't fulfill the happiness we are in search of, so we try again. We work hard and make more money. We invest in high ticket items that we believe will bring joy in our lives, will make us more comfortable, and will finally allow us to be happy. But we're not.

Maybe we are looking in the wrong direction. The balance we all need to seek begins in the inside of us, it does not lay in the material world. Balance is a feeling we get when we are relaxed. You wouldn't find this by scratching your way to the top of your career field and you won't find it by trying to satisfy your desires of having more toys than anyone else. Morgan hit a patch in her life that continued to take her down, one anxiety at a time, until she had spiraled out of control and hit bottom.

We have a tendency to look to our external world for answers to finding true peace, tranquility, and balance in our life. We plan vacation cruises or look to buy that new living room suite or worse yet, go in debt to obtain a new boat or a new car all as an attempt to gain prestige and happiness. Instead of looking to others or the outside world to make us feel good, feel important, or to boost our self esteem, we need to be looking into the mirror for our own acceptance first and foremost. It seems that we keep sabotaging our own efforts by not stopping to realize what true happiness is. We need to stay focused on our inner self first, then once established we will have the ability to assess our needs and desires in a rational and loving pursuit of life's happiness.

Are you trapped by the expectations of society? Are you trading in your values for a reputation? You are free to make any choice that you want in your life but you need to ensure that you are doing so while also being knowledgeable of the consequences for your actions. You just may be trading in any chance of discovering harmony in your life or feeling the true inner peace and happiness that you feel you are lacking.

A fast pace – have it all attitude can make you miserable. Balance is hard to find when you are so busy trying to survive, that you can't take the time needed for yourself and your inner core that grants you calmness and stability. You might franticly jump from one thing to the next never taking the time to let any thoughts of doubt enter your mind. Then one day out of the blue, there is quiet, and as you look around at your worldly goods you suddenly feel a twinge inside tugging at your heart. You can't decipher what sensation this is. You spend days, weeks, maybe months, carrying around this feeling that you can't identify. You are discontent and somewhat frustrated, then suddenly you have an epiphany, you couldn't identify the feeling because the feeling is of emptiness, a void that is telling you that something is missing in your life.

By looking only at our external world, we all tend to build an illusion in our minds as to how to identify happiness and successes. We are more concerned as to how others may view us, rather than looking within and gauging our happiness and success on the ability to view the world and nature that surrounds us and the capacity to love and be loved.

Perception is the process of acquiring, interpreting, selecting, and organizing sensory information. It is important to understand perception and the way that you view life events, including the things that happen in your immediate surroundings. In changing a negative perception you need to defuse that thought process which would have normally caused negative reactions. Emotions are great if they are positive emotions such as happiness, joy, excitement, or contentment. Negative emotions cause the turmoil that throw you off kilter and cause you to be, do, or say irrational things.

"Change your thoughts and you change your world."
-Norman Vincent Peale

Your thoughts are what make up the world that you live in. You could place the blame for all your fears or negative outlook on life on your parents, an abusive relationship, being abandoned, being raised in an unhealthy environment, or many other numerous reasons but it all boils down to the here and now. You will need to identify with what has led you to this point in your life but you don't need to dwell on it or seek revenge for any of your misfortunes. One of the many things you will learn is the need to forgive and to let go of all negative thoughts and this you will accomplish through new knowledge. At this point in time you are knowledgeable that changes can be made if you are willing to make them. Your life is now in your hands, you have the ability to turn everything around. Of course you are not going to do this with one big change but with many small changes moving one step at a time.

Sometimes we unknowingly are stuck living in the past, rather the present. When we have been hurt by someone in our past, we can place barriers all around us for protection, we are fearful of forgiving and letting go. In doing this you successfully molded the past and the future into one so that you are always living in the past. We tend to view things negatively when something has occurred that alters or disrupts our lives, simply because it is unexpected and therefore an inconvenience. Negativity will only hinder the efforts of finding an acceptable solution. By always looking at the negative side, you will find that you can easily double or triple your worry.

When working through the pain of past experiences in preparation to move forward, you need to take a clear look at where you are currently in your life then evaluate how your past experiences still affect you today. You will be preparing to create new building blocks that, one by one, will replace the negative or undesirable responses you have learned in your attempts to protect yourself from pain.

Picking out negative aspects of your life will not be an easy task but without acknowledging these behaviors you won't be able to change your perception of what prompts these reactions. Our emotions are a product of our thoughts and perceptions, so these will be your targets of improvement. As it took many years to adapt these negative behaviors it will also take time, trust, and baby steps to turn these situations around. Seeking help and choosing a path of recovery is essential to future growth and victory over these crippling emotions. It is time to let go of the past and step into your future.

When looking back in an attempt to understand your weaknesses, look closely at issues of self esteem. Self image is how you feel others view you. Perception of a negative self image is shown in your actions and words. You may feel inadequate and have no self confidence in your own abilities. You may view yourself as unworthy of acceptance and consistently feel as though you don't fit in anywhere you go or with anything that you do. These are the feelings that you mirror to others. Low self esteem can rob you of any hopes or goals for the future and you may even find it exhausting to even try to come up with any if you have fallen into a stage of helplessness and no longer have any enthusiasm for life.

(Joyce Myer,1995, 41) "Positive minds produce positive lives. Negative minds produce negative lives. Positive thoughts are always full of faith and hope. Negative thoughts are always full of fear and doubt." The time to start making your personal changes is now. There is no need to look for another job, career, relationship, or even another chance at living the life you envision until we make the changes that need to be made. Changing where you are geographically has no bearing on personal change. If we go into new situations with the same attitude and outlook on life then you will see the same results over and over again. If you want the circumstances to change then you need to gather your lessons from the past and then set them to the side and move forward with a new perspective, new beliefs and a new attitude.

Negativity as a way of viewing life can be developed in situations where you are or were subjected to chronic stress. Examples may be living in an abusive home life or it could be a place of employment. Regardless of the condition, the most effective action you would think would be to remove yourself from the environment causing the stress. This isn't impossible, but many times it's not the most desirable immediate remedy and could generate other undesirable ramifications. To make a life-altering change requires you to take time and contemplate your actions using problem solving techniques and reviewing the possible outcomes of your actions. In the meantime you need to identify your own strengths and build confidence in yourself. The meditation example given under visualization in chapter 8 will be of great help in this area.

Attribution theory simply stated, speculates how individuals explain actions, behaviors or situations whether it be theirs or another's. This hinges on variables such as perception and self-image. People have a natural instinct or reaction to judge others actions and defend their own. Perception covers a wide span of territory as it takes into consideration someone's attitude and personality, this being dependant on their outlook of themselves and the world.

When we have a negative outlook either of ourselves or the outer world, you place more stress into your life as you continue to battle your own pessimistic attitude. Positive thinking gives you a more confident and secure self image and in turn yields more happiness in your direction.

The attribution theory was developed by Fritz Heider and his colleagues and looks at two different ways in which individuals would explain why things happen.

(Heider, 1959)

- External – means the cause is due to an outside force and therefore the individual themselves are not at fault.
- Internal – means that you accept personal responsibility and place the cause of your actions upon yourself.

Although the attribution theory observes that all behavior results from both external and internal forces, we have a tendency to lean more towards one direction or the other in our explanations.

If I say to you, "You're a bad driver." Are you going to say to me, "Yea, I guess I could use some good tips for driving" or are you going to say something like "You are just a nervous passenger" or maybe blame it on the weather. Chances are you will defend your ego and self image by redirecting any blame of bad driving away from you and place it on an outside factor to deflect you being sited as the cause of bad driving.

If on the other hand I say to you, "This presentation that you developed is outstanding." Would you be more likely to take personal responsibility based on your knowledge and skills that you contributed to its success or would you place the cause on an outside factor such as chance or an unplanned success.

The attribution theory would lay odds that you would contribute your success to being caused by your own knowledge, skills, and abilities and if you experienced a miscalculation that resulted in an error, that you would then contribute this to an outside factor such as you were given the wrong information. In defense of our own image, if an adversary were to have succeeded you may credit it to luck or an accident.

It is time to drop your defenses and enjoy life. The energy that you spend in your defense can be better spent elsewhere. We are all human and we don't have to be perfect at everything we do. Open your heart and mind into accepting other people's opinions and share your thoughts, gain knowledge from others, and give knowledge. By setting up strong defenses you are placing a wall between you and the rest of the world, this action does not allow for the exchange of information that is so valuable to learn from.

To build self-esteem in an individual, it is important to compliment them on their strengths and to initiate positive feedback on their accomplishments. Your current analysis of your own self-esteem levels may be positive or negative and either way this is based on past and/or current experiences. If subjected to a mentally abusive atmosphere where you were degraded and made to feel useless, you most likely are dealing with a low self esteem. If you have been fortunate to be surrounded by supportive friends and family members that encourage your success by positive feedback and compliments, then they have been instrumental in helping you build a solid foundation for a positive, successful self image.

We seek approval and build self-esteem from many sources that are outside of us. This is a natural reaction and is beneficial unless we build our whole world around how others view us. If we do a good job or make a good decision and someone corroborates our thoughts then our strength and image of ourselves is reinforced. As you give, so shall you receive. The best way to feel good about you is to help another. Share your words and your thoughts to make someone else feel appreciated just for being there, nothing more. Positive thinking and the power of words are free but more valuable than gold when you are looking for acceptance and confidence.

When someone comes to you maybe at work and tells you, "You do an outstanding job!" how does this make you feel? This builds your confidence and you feel pretty good and proud of yourself, right? We all try to be outstanding; we all seek the approval of others to give a boost to our self-esteem. But many times, in this way to busy world, people don't stop to take the time to give someone a pat on the back and let them know just how special they are. This is where you come in.

If you take the time to let someone know how special they are, what do they do? They try even harder, because now they have a goal, a self image to live up to and something to strive harder for to surpass. For example, you are hired for a job and work hard to show that you are worthy of your position and are capable of bigger and better things. Months go by and you are treated with negativity or indifference, like you are invisible. Naturally, your enthusiasm plummets and your performance declines. This happens when you haven't been given the opportunity to build self-esteem based on positive feedback that is needed for the motivation of growth.

If a child brings home a good grade from class and you show them your excitement and let them know what an excellent achievement they have made, what is their reaction? You not only boost their self image but you can be sure that the next good grade they get, they come running home to show you. Everyone yearns for those positive words of confidence, whether you are a child or an adult we all like to be recognized.

Most don't consider the power of words and how they can change someone's life. Everyone likes to hear how other people feel about them, considering that they are good comments anyway. Telling someone they are wonderful, they are excellent at what they do, or even a simple compliment on how they look is all it takes to give a miracle. You will gain the acceptance and respect of many and in turn will boost your own self esteem by helping others.

The power of your words can change someone's life. It can give confidence where they were lacking, support when they are in need, friendship when they feel alone or attention when they feel unnoticed. A complete stranger is waiting for you to reach out your hand and make them feel special. Everyone desires the approval that you hold in your words. Try it today with anyone and watch the light of hope and happiness that you bring into someone's world.

Some individuals tend to walk forward and view the world with tunnel vision, they are focused on too many tasks of their own and miss the human factor of life, the sharing, the caring, and the support that we need to build self-esteem in each other.

If you are harboring a low self image of yourself then you have been taught feelings of worthlessness such as being unwanted, unloved, or unworthy to experience, or even hope for anything good to happen in your life. (Jampolsky, 1979) Gerald Jampolsky, M.D. in his book, 'Love Is Letting Go of Fear' stated that, "If we are willing, it is possible to change our belief system. However, to do so we must take a new look at every one of our cherished assumptions and values from the past. This means letting go of any investment in holding on to fear, anger, guilt or pain. It means letting the past slip away and with it all the fears from the past that we keep extending into the present and future."

Self evaluation can uncover characteristics that you may not have noticed or maybe viewed as irrelevant in your journey to unravel your past and place balance in your life. A habit is an acquired pattern of behavior that often occurs automatically, without being provoked by thought. This occurs with repetitive behavior over a length of time. Because of this automatic response, you may not be consciously aware that you are displaying negative behavior or having negative thoughts until your focus is directed to this area of your life.

To change any negative perceptions of yourself or the world you must be willing to acknowledge the current way that you view these areas of your life. Be honest with yourself and be willing to examine alternative positive views to replace these perceptions. Change is never easy. It is always more comfortable to stay within the boundaries of what is familiar, rather than step out into the unknown. It's time to open your wings and prepare to fly. You will be required to take risks as you unwrap yourself from your safe cocoon and join the world. To dispel fears will mean to acknowledge them and then change your perception of what is making you fearful.

The first place to start is to review how you perceive yourself, how do you relate to others, your relationships, love, and family? Keep in mind that any imperfections that you may have developed you built out of fear. Fear that you were not good enough, fear that nobody could love you, fear that your thoughts were of no importance to anyone else. Every negative imperfection that you note, will lead you back to your fears. The negative perceptions need to be altered and replaced with neutral or positive perceptions.

How many times do you find that you make negative comments of yourself? "I'm too old," "I'm too young," "I'm too fat," "Why do I always mess things up," "I feel so inadequate," "I can't do anything right," "I'm so slow," and the list goes on. Your image of yourself has a way of dictating how you feel and how you react to your environment. (Bradshaw, 1988, [a] 191) John Bradshaw wrote a book titled 'Healing the Shame that Binds You' in which he states that, "Shame inducing thoughts tend to fall into three categories: self put-downs; catastrophic thoughts about one's inability to handle the future; and critical and shaming thoughts of remorse and regrets. The "if only" I hadn't done such and such are sure ways to trigger shame spirals. And self put downs like, "I'm too shy to make friends or get what I need," or "I'm so stupid," are ways to trigger shame spirals. Obsessions about your failures and limitations trigger spirals, resulting in severe depression."

These thoughts are self defeating and self destructive, for instance, if you think negatively about yourself such as "I'm so stupid," then chances are if working on a project, you won't give your undivided attention to the project, you will assume in the long run your efforts will be un-noticed or perceived as a failure, so you will say things to yourself such as, "this won't be accepted by others, it's just a waste of my time," or "there are so many people that could do the job better than me." You will work so hard at not succeeding that you will eventually prove that your own expectation of yourself was correct and unknowingly reinforce your negative behaviors.

Would you have felt or acted any differently while doing this same project if your thoughts were more like, "I can do anything if I put all of my effort into it," "Practice makes perfect," or "If I work hard and refuse to give up, I can succeed." Our perceptions and expectations will ultimately guide us to the end result of our product.

- Do you have negative thoughts about yourself?
- Do you condemn yourself more than pat yourself on the back for a job well done?
- Are you always bracing yourself for the worst outcome?
- How often do you view the negative in a person rather than focus on the positive?
- If you have 100 compliments and 1 criticism which one do you dwell on?

Below you will find four perception challenges that will help you determine how your thought process currently works.

Challenge 1 - Throughout the next few days, pay attention to how many times a negative thought comes into your mind or a negative statement about yourself comes out of your mouth. You may discover that you are harder on yourself than you thought.

When you are working on altering your perceptions of yourself, you need to understand why you are having the negative thoughts. Chances are likely that these thoughts are due to some hidden fear that you believe about yourself. Negativity and fear drain your energy and make you weak. This weakness will make you lose faith in yourself. Each time you catch yourself making a negative statement about yourself, stop and ask yourself, "What caused me to say that?"

Using this technique, you are working from your current observation backwards, to find what has triggered the thought. Keep asking yourself why until you get down to the root of the fear, until you get a final, bottom-of-the-barrel answer. This is a form of constructive self-examination that you will find useful dealing with everyday stresses that are involved with your self confidence. You may not want to admit what the true fear is but you are the only person who will know and benefit from this truth, so be honest. Once you have identified these fears you will be able to work at overcoming them by altering your perception.

Instead of saying, "I can't do anything right." Replace this with, "I can do anything I set my mind to, with determination and patience." Instead of saying, "I am so fat," replace this with, "I think I want to start changing my eating habits." Instead of, "Nobody likes me," replace this with, "I'm going to work on letting people get to know and understand me." Any negative thought that you catch replace this with a positive thought. Inside you are locked secrets of who you truly are, as you peal back the layers and shed the negativity from your life the true you, the happy and positive you, will surface.

If you are finding it hard to alter your perception when it comes to your insecurities that you have of yourself, try this exercise to help strengthen your self confidence.

- Jot key notes on a piece of paper. Note accomplishments you have made in your life beginning from your school awards and accomplishments when you were younger, through your more current accomplishments and successes no matter how small or big. Record anything that has made you proud.
- Read a copy of your job resume if you have one, to acknowledge the progress you have made in your life, and look at how you have grown and what you have learned over the years.
- Make a list of your strengths, everything you can think of. List things that you enjoy doing and list things that you feel you're really good at.

Now look at the list and reevaluate your self image and confidence. Sometimes, when we doubt our own capabilities, we blind ourselves to our strengths and accomplishments. Everyone, even the most intelligent, popular, successful people have weaknesses but they focus on their strengths because this is what they know they can succeed at, then they learn and expand their knowledge as they grow.

Other methods available for building self-esteem, self image, and confidence of your own can be accomplished by means of meditation and visualization. This can change a negative perception of ones self to a positive image to build on. (See Chapter 8 for relaxation exercises)

Challenge 2 – Just for one day commit in your mind that you are going to be non-judgmental with every person you come into contact with. That's not to say that you have to love them or be in agreement with everything that they say, you just cannot judge what they say, how they look, live, or view the world.

Notice how many times you start to judge in your mind and you have to pull your thoughts back to your commitment. Being judgmental not only places negativity in your mind but carries this over into future thoughts. "When under an illusion of insight," Dr. William J, Knaus (1994), says "your intuition dominates. You decide about people's character based on first impressions and never suspect you are wrong. You base your decision on how you feel at the time."

A judgmental person will be judged. When we abstain from negative thinking and judgment and replace this with compassion and caring, the same will be reflected back to us.

Challenge 3 – Open your eyes and your ears with the people you come into contact with or who call you on the phone. Really listen to what they are saying. Have you ever known someone who is constantly on the verge of crisis, someone who always has to be the center of attention like with the Queen Bee syndrome, someone who is overbearing, impatient, or rude?

Have you listened to conversations or engaged in conversations in which the other person is constantly saying negative things? Keep your mind focused to pick up on these occurrences for a day. Note how much negativity is around you in your environment, then pull away from these negative situations and don't let yourself be drawn into them.

Negativity in your surroundings is contagious you can get pulled into a conversation and find yourself agreeing with someone who is speaking negatively about another, about their job, or about life in general. If you are agreeing because you just don't want to be bothered with the conversation, then walk away, if you are agreeing because you fear confrontation of stating how you really feel, walk away You don't want their negative image to attach itself to you.

You need to keep your distance from negative individuals until you are strong enough to make your positive thinking known to others and step up to plate to speak your thoughts. You would be amazed at how the conversation quiets when someone is speaking negatively and you refuse to join in their misery. When you don't support their way of thinking, the negative person unless they are confrontational, will shut up and the others that were thinking the same as you are now all of a sudden nodding in agreement and interjecting positive words of their own.

Challenge 4 - Lastly, observe the way someone looks when they are being rude or impatient. What characteristics shine through when you are looking at the person who is unsatisfied, discontent, and negative? Observe their facial expressions, now visualize how you must appear to other people when you are caught up in these negative behaviors. Is it an appealing picture?

If you want to have a charismatic personality, one that stands above the rest, then controlling stress and eliminating negativity are important factors to alter your character and develop a unique personality that people value and respect. Positive thinking will draw others towards you as they realize that being positive and being around positive people makes them feel so much better and encourages a more enjoyable atmosphere.

Successful relationships and interaction skills are based on our perception and how we choose to view any given situation either negatively or positively. Your perception of an event depends on your emotional state of mind at the time that the event occurs. If you feel strong and competent you will reflect that in your reaction. If you are feeling tired and weak you will reflect the same. We control how we react depending on how we feel and how we choose to contemplate a situation.

Altering your perception to focus and utilize positive thoughts, will reduce your frustration and in turn reduce your stress. By controlling how you perceive any given situation you can control your reaction to the situation. Example, you are at work and trying to help a customer to resolve an issue such as returning a piece of merchandise or straightening out an account that this person has accidentally been over charged on. This person is frustrated and displacing those feelings onto you.

If you view this person as inconsiderate, hostile, and rude you will react in your own defense to this person, which will trigger your flight-or-fight response. You may be able to foresee that this reaction will only result in a negative outcome. If on the other hand, you consider altering your perception of this incident and view this person as insecure and confused, which is the cause of this person's outburst, then your reaction will be more reassuring, supportive, and accommodating. This then is the more positive and desirable result. Altering your perception of the world around you by using thought controls will help to apply a more caring demeanor when responding to others.

If you are dealing with another individual one on one that is causing you to feel stress building, then even though you may not be able to retreat to a different location, use any excuse to turn away (for example, reach behind you for a piece of paper or look in a drawer to locate a pen) and regain control of the situation. This is a good time to use your breathing technique. Remember, you can choose how to react, and this is not only a challenge but an opportunity to practice calming effects and maintaining control.

Nobody can steal your peace, unless you choose to surrender it to them.

Our minds are very powerful. Thought control techniques are a process and a skill that can be developed which allows you to alter your perception of a particular situation at any given moment. We have the ability, just by implanting a certain thought in our mind, to feel the emotions that are associated with that thought. Once you understand the process you can train your mind to respond in a controlled manner of your choice, depending on what seed you plant.

Follow this exercise to recognize and identify the difference between a thought and an emotion. Once you recognize the two as separate entities, you will be able to manipulate your thoughts and disconnect yourself from any negative response.

It is a matter of rotating your thoughts, moving them from one visualization to another. When you shift visualizations, take the time to note the emotional response you have to your thought before you move forward to the next thought. You will achieve best results if you associate your thoughts with actual experiences from your past that generated these feelings. Take your time with each thought to recapture the feelings that you felt at this particular time.

STRESS AND THOUGHT CONTROL EXERCISE

- Think a calming thought, perhaps of a time that you were very relaxed and at peace with yourself. Maybe when you were lying on the beach or camping out in nature. (Take the time to visualize your thought and note your emotional response that is attached to the visualization.)

- Think of a time when someone, maybe a parent or a friend, was very angry with you and said some hurtful things. How did you feel?
- Think of a loving time, maybe a walk hand in hand with someone you love.
- Think of a time when someone made you feel extraordinarily important, perhaps when you won an award or got a promotion.
- Think of a time and how it made you feel when someone degraded you, maybe by saying to you, "You're so stupid." Or maybe a time when some kids picked on you and called you names when you were young.
- Lastly, think of a time when you laughed so hard that your side ached and you thought you were going to cry.

You should have noticed that by planting a different seed in your mind, and taking the time to relate to that thought, you had an emotional reaction that immediately attached itself to that memory. We can learn to use our minds this way to help us with our everyday challenges. You can control your thoughts with practice.

Pick a couple of very calming memories and/or happy memories of your past and embed them in your mind for easy retrieval if you should need to call on them. If it is better for you to keep a constant reminder at your fingertips until you use this technique routinely, place a marble in your pocket, a picture on your desk, or some similar idea to alert you of the need to keep your focus on these calming thoughts when necessary.

Learn to use the above technique when someone triggers your stress response. When you begin to experience your breathing quicken and your blood pressure rise, bring back to mind one of these memories. Use your breathing techniques and your thought controls to regain power in any stressful situation. (See Chapter 8 for breathing techniques.)

Things will go wrong in your life that is inevitable. My question would be, "How do you plan to react when things don't go your way?" We of course, all have a choice as to how we respond to any given situation, "Do you respond by focusing on the negative or do you respond by focusing on the positive?" There is a balance in all facets of life and there is a balance with positive and negative energy, with any situation. We can be drawn towards looking at the negative aspects or we can make the choice of being drawn towards the positive thinking aspects.

In our lives if you stop to think about it we always have at the minimum of two choices in everything we do. Back in school we learned of Newton's physical law, the law states that with every action there is an equal and opposite reaction and therefore every cause has an effect. Equal and opposite reactions consist of things such as the choices, up versus down, in versus out, positive or negative, dark or light, over or short, happy or sad, good and evil, heaven and hell, stop or go, left or right, you can see my point.

You will need to make your choice to embrace the positive and discard the negative. The personalities that we develop are a product of how we choose to view life in general. Without the knowledge that we have these choices, it is easy to drift in the wrong direction. Our challenge then is to control our thoughts so that we always understand at any given moment in time – we have a choice, on how we think, on how we react, on how we choose to live this one life we have been given.

We cannot back up in time and change the bad choices we made yesterday but we can choose today to grasp the knowledge that we have learned and move forward making the choices that not only make us happy, but will also help every life we come in contact with. You have the power to make amazing changes in your life and in those lives that you touch. Only you hold the power to make these choices and these choices will effect every hour of every day that passes as you develop the new you.

You will always find it beneficial if you view the many sides to each issue before jumping to a decision. Study management and leadership skills. Even if you are not in this type of position they are always focused on positive thinking, making your customers happy, understanding the personalities of employees and how to address negative behavior. There is an old time goodie that probably every person who has been in a management position remembers, it's called 'The One Minute Manager,' this book originally came out in 1982 (also available in CD format), since then the 'Leadership and the One Minute Manager' has taken front stage. These are great resources to keep around you to refer to for a boost of energy while adapting to your new outlook on life.

Like a resume you need to keep focused on your strengths not your weaknesses. Look at all of the beauty that surrounds you. Take the time to enjoy life's small pleasures as well as the large ones. Take pride in what you contribute to this world – generate passion and give purpose to every task you take on.

Let's use a brief example on how your thoughts, positive and negative along with your attitude can dictate what you achieve in life.

Let's say you have an appointment scheduled for a job interview. You wake up that morning and you think, "I'll never get that job, why am I even wasting my time going to this interview?" You have no motivation. You arrive at the interview and you give off those negative vibes of discontentment and low self esteem. Do you think this is the type of person you would hire?

But Lets say you wake up that morning and your excitement of a new goal and anticipation of how you are going to excel at this new position is bubbling over. You are excited as you dress for the interview and arrive 15 minutes early so you can get a feel of the new environment.

Be realistic… which individual would you hire. Even if the negative person had more previous experience, you want the enthusiastic, upbeat go getter that is self confident, motivated, and has a zest for life's experiences.

By using positive thinking you eliminate the stress that negative thinking can place on you. Negative thinking will always be a dark cloud that travels overhead. Everyone who meets you will be repelled by the negativity. The law of attraction weighs heavily on both sides. If you are negative – negativity can squeeze the breath out of you, but if you see the positive side of life the positive will fill you up so that you fly high above the rest.

Have you ever heard it said, "When one door closes another one opens"? When a part of our life has been altered, especially when we did not anticipate or want the change to occur, it's natural to want to hang on to what once was for fear of letting go of something familiar and this definitely appears safer than change. We tend to stall, so to speak, we get so fixated on what we want (behind the closed door), that we never turn to look in the other direction to see what door may have opened and what opportunities may lie ahead. Being a positive thinker assures that you will always look with open eyes to the possibilities of the future.

Sometimes you may be able to lessen your stress by defining your perceptions and expectations that you have of yourself, others and the world around you. Once you have a clear picture of your potential and opportunities that you may want to pursue this can generate some satisfaction and ambition to create some pleasures to look forward to and strive to attain.

Have you ever considered that you may need to define what happiness truly is to you? Sometimes we may not be able to define if we are happy, sad or indifferent because we haven't begun to define what it is we want to accomplish in life, we haven't set any goals. We are just floating from one day to the next and waiting for something to happen to us that strikes change in our life.

As stated by Dr. William J, Knaus (1994), "Behind d-stress (destructive stress) we find many conflicts between imagination and reality that often involve one or more of several misconceptions: Life should be fair; you should have what you want; you should have complete control over who you want to be or what you want to do; what was shouldn't have been. To find the illusions behind your d-stress, look for some unreasonable expectations about life."

"When the same unfortunate things happen to you," says Dr. Knaus (1994), "chances are an illusion is behind the turmoil. Look at the gaps in your life – what you want to accomplish, and can accomplish, but avoid. Sometimes seeing what is missing in your life opens the blinds to discovering an illusion that interferes with the purposeful changes you would normally choose to make."

There has been much research on happiness. Throughout history and in different cultures individuals have tried to dissect and give scientific feedback about this jolly feeling. What is it? How does it work? Where does it come from? What does it mean? Many have stated their opinion of how they define this word or feeling.

It's my turn so this is my opinion:

Although you may be able to define it, it is not something you can see or touch, it is inside of you. When searching for it, only you can determine whether it will be found.

Some individuals I believe think that it is something that jumps out in front of them and they walk right smack into it. It just appears, and if it doesn't just appear they feel cheated and abandoned. "What's wrong with me?" "Why didn't I get any?"

I dread to tell you but I don't believe that you will walk smack into it and it's not something that jumps out of the darkness. It is what we do each day that determines the amount of happiness that we experience.

We tend to take the things that make us smile for granted but these are the things that happen in our every day life that if you don't stop to acknowledge them in that moment, then it goes un-noticed. If it goes un-noticed then who is to say that it ever happened. Therefore, even if there are many moments of happiness in your life it becomes invisible to your heart.

You need to enjoy these priceless pleasures when they occur, then do the same for the next small token of joy that makes you smile and so on. Then as you stop to smell the roses, so to speak, every time a tidbit of happiness passes you by, these nuggets will start to link one to another forming a noticeable string of happiness. Not every moment of every day will you be bursting with joy but to feel happiness, we need to stop and acknowledge those things that bring us joy. Finding your joy is determined by how you perceive your life.

(Bradshaw, 1988, 196) "Overgeneralizations lead to universal qualifiers like, "Nobody loves me ... I'll never get a better job ... I will always have to struggle ... Why can't I ever get it right? ... No one would love me if they really knew me ..." Other cue words are all, every, and everybody. Overgeneralizations contribute to a greater and greater restricted lifestyle. They present a grandiose absolutizing, which implies that some immutable law governs your chances of happiness." As we know this is not true since we are responsible for our own actions and creating our own happiness. This is why letting go of the past and any hurtful or demoralizing perceptions you had of yourself is essential to regaining the control over your life.

If you seem to experience more sadness, frustration, and dread in your days then you do moments of joy, then most likely there is something in your life that weighs heavy on your heart and mind creating this bourdon of sadness. To release this sadness you first need to find out what's generating it and make a decision as to how you are going to start changing this area of your life. Identifying your unhappiness and making adjustments in your life will allow you to sweep away all of the cobwebs so that you can not only see but feel the happiness you are depriving yourself of.

Take the time now to stop and analyze the larger portions of your life. Are you satisfied when you are at home, when you are at work, with family and friends, with the activities that you participate in, or with the significant other that may be involved in your life? This is where you will find the area of your life that you will need to place your focus for improvement. After you determine the area of sadness, don't in one swoop eliminate this from your life thinking this will resolve your sadness. Sometimes the harder you try to control events, the less likely they are to be controlled. Quick decisions are not thought out decisions and when you act on a whim this can compound the issue you are trying to resolve.

Break this area into smaller bits to zoom in on what the core of the problem is. If it is your home life then determine what in your home life exactly is making you unhappy. For example, if you determine that you don't like the physical location of your home, then your focus needs to be on, "Where do I want to live?" Take your time and think about all of the different possibilities. Write them down so you can see every opportunity that is in your mind. See yourself in each one of these scenarios.

When you determine where you truly want to be then you'll need to make a small goal that will start you headed in that direction. Don't view the whole picture at one time, this will only overwhelm you and then you may give up before you even start. Set reasonable small goals to get you focused in that direction. One little step forward will start the momentum needed to continue moving forward. While working on taking that first step, take the time to contemplate what the next step will be. After the first step is accomplished, focus on completing the second step and determine what your third step will be and so on.

To balance areas in your life you have to make changes. This takes thought and this takes logical thinking. This means you'll need to make a plan to get away from your surroundings for a day or two and make some plans to get your life back to a healthy balance. Meditation and silence is the goal you need to commit to. You need to develop an atmosphere that allows you to relax. You will find that giving rational advice is easier if you are giving advice to another individual, in other words take yourself out of the equation to view things from a more distant perspective. Give yourself the advice you would recommend to another. You need to listen to the rational part of you to find the answers and create the balance.

Unhappiness can cause feelings of frustration and anger that can affect many areas of your life, whether in your personal relationships or work relations and can pile on stress but change doesn't happen the moment you know what you want. It just places your thoughts in that direction so that you can strategize how you want to get there. Having inner peace helps you use a rational thought process to reach deep within yourself to search for your true feelings.

Inner peace is something else that only you can give yourself. It's nothing you can buy and it's nothing that you can get from anyone else, it is something you experience from deep within when you have an open and loving heart. It will reflect your character, it will be the basis of your morals and values that you hold dear to you. When you are looking for an answer you may take outside variables into consideration but you will then look within to determine your final actions. Listening is the source of finding peace and knowing that you are on the correct path. (Jampolsky, 1979, 65) "Inner peace can be reached only when we practice forgiveness. Forgiveness is the vehicle for changing our perceptions and letting go of our fears, condemning judgments and grievances."

We all have voices in our head that we listen to. There is a tiny voice and there is a big voice. Sometimes you listen to the little voice and sometimes you listen to the big voice and sometimes you don't listen at all. Maybe you weren't sure what voice to listen to. Chances are that you should have listened to the smaller voice. There is a difference between the big voice and the little voice and this is the first step to understanding.

When God created us he placed that little voice in us hoping it would drown out the big voice as we matured, learned and carried on our life. It is a little piece of him inside of us, 'God's will' that guides us through our lifetime and contributes to our inner peace. If you can make that voice grow you will always find yourself on the right path. The big voice that is very hard to drown out is called your ego. Your ego has a very close friend called Id (the self gratifying part of you) and Id is always out for self gratification and pleasure.

(Williamson, 1992, 36) "The ego is our mental power turned against ourselves. It is clever, like we are, and smooth talking, like we are, and manipulative, like we are. The ego doesn't come up to us and say, "Hi, I'm your self-loathing." Rather it says things like, "Hi, I'm your adult, mature, rational self. I'll help you look out for number one." Then it proceeds to counsel us to look out for ourselves, at the expense of others. It teaches us selfishness, greed, judgment, and small-mindedness."

To understand this to the fullest here is a short story that will leave you with full understanding of inner peace and the voices within.

There was a boy who wanted to buy a used car so that he didn't have to take the bus to work every day and he would be able to cruise with his friends and bathe in their envy. He was barley able to make ends meet while paying his own living expenses.

One day he was lucky in a drawing that awarded him $2,000 dollars. This was just enough money to buy that used car that he wanted. He called the dealership to see if the car was still available and it was. He couldn't wait to jump on the bus and speed to the dealership with his money. As he opened his door and ran out he scared a small kitten lying in his grass. The kitten was skin and bones, hair matted, and although startled, did not have the strength to run. He just wobbled back and forth as he tried to stand up.

The boy picked up the kitten knowing there was a vet on his way. He thought he could at least drop off the kitten so the vet could put him out of his misery. The little voice inside him was squirming and whispering, "This fragile life wants love, warmth and to live." The big voice was saying "This is going to cost you hundreds at the vet and that will certainly set you back on getting that car that would be the envy of your friends." The little voice says "Let's just go and talk with the vet and see what he'll charge, we can always get a less expensive car."

Although the big voice was so strong the little voice won because the boy had connected with his inner peace as the little life that was held in the boys hand became more important. Sometimes that little voice is not easy to recognize. Also, when the ego and his friend, 'Id' catch on to the fact that their losing out a lot they may try to disguise themselves as a little voice, anything to trick you. Inner peace can be recognized when you feel good about the choices that you make.

There are three basic words you learned for safety when you were little. Now, they can really help you out at this juncture in your life. They are *Stop, Look* and *Listen*. That boy with the kitten took the time to Stop. He could have just jumped onto the bus and drove away, thinking the kitten wasn't his nor was it his problem. When he would return the kitten would be gone. Stopping, gave him the time he needed to look within and listen to the voices. He could have just dropped the kitten at the vet's doorstep to have him put to sleep and go buy his car, or pay the vet, make the kitten better, and get a less expensive car.

By *Stopping* and *looking* he had reached the most vital step in his growth. He took the time to decipher what voice to *listen* to. Although he had to take a loss at getting the used car he had his heart set on, he now has a kitten that will forever show love and gratitude. He doesn't need friends to envy him that was only his ego wanting center stage.

Many individuals, mostly during trying times, question their existence as they search for the meaning of Life? This is a stressful event that can throw you into a downward spiral sending you deeper and deeper into a depressive state of mind. You constantly question, "Why was I placed here on this earth" "What am I suppose to be doing?"

Every time you think you have found the way and are on the right path, an explosion hits and the path in front of you has been blocked. It's painful to keep getting mentally beat up when you are trying to find your way in this world and just when you think it is within your grasp – everything changes and you're back to square one, wondering what to do and where to go from here.

STOP…LOOK…LISTEN

At this stage of the book, you should have some thoughts on the directions and issues you would like to focus on for change. You have the capacity to determine where you would like your life to go. Stop a moment and think … what are your joys you have gathered in life … what experiences have you had … what do you love to do more than anything else…what are your passions? Having a positive attitude, finding your passion and living your dreams however large or small they are, can be the meaning of your life. Once you start living your passion, you will view life with contentment and happiness knowing all is right in the world.

Dr. William J, Knaus (1994), says "People like to do what they can do well. You excel when you concentrate on what is profitable, where you have talent, and where you work hard at what comes easiest."

I have a sign on my wall to remind me that I need to keep on those paths. It says, "May today there be peace within you. May you trust God that you are exactly where you are meant to be." I don't know where it came from or who said it, it's been there for years but by using this sign, my inner peace and positive thinking, I found my passion, my meaning to life and I can keep focused on the path ahead.

To discover your passion focus on what you like about yourself, as well as the things that you do in life that you enjoy. What have other people throughout your life acknowledged to you that you are good at? If you enjoy something, you have a passion about this subject and this passion can develop into a part of your individual uniqueness. There is a natural balance created within the world and we need every person and their gifts and skills that they were given before birth, to make the balance work to our advantage. The more people that find their uniqueness or gift, the more we decrease the gap and bring the balance of the world in closer harmony. How to find what valuable gift you have to offer in this world is the secret within yourself, so unlock your passion.

We all have gifts to offer. You may be an outstanding parent that devotes your life to raising your children, to teach them and others that surround you strong values and morals. You teach individuals through example how to respect the lives of others, to set high standards and goals and to excel at what they are good at. You are the beacon of light for others to find their way. This is my sister's passion and God needs her in this position.

Maybe you find you can communicate well with the elderly and you love to make them smile and assist them with coping with life and their difficulties. You may love working and tinkering with automobiles, working with animals, bringing knowledge to others to make their lives less complicated, or providing a service to the people in your community. It could be reading books, cleaning house, talking on the phone, or you may be a great organizer. Whatever you find your passion to be, coping with life should not become a burden, it should be a journey to find this passion and create the life that you love waking up to each and every day. Think about it. What if nobody in the world liked to build houses – we would be living in tents and huts. What if nobody liked to stock grocery shelves, to file papers, to cook --- you get my point. We need to enjoy what we do and give back to the world that we live in.

Living your passion could lead you towards financial freedom, happiness, contentment, self-determination, independence, but most of all and most important, you will have developed your individual uniqueness that helps bring balance into the world that surrounds you and this talent that God gave you is your salvation, your purpose and your significance for being placed on this earth. I for one am so glad that you are here. Thank you for what you do and for everything that you are going to do with your future.

When you learn how to identify your negative behaviors and take the necessary steps to correct these self-limiting behaviors, you will experience remarkable changes in your life, boundaries will be limitless, your mind will be at peace and in harmony with your body, you will achieve things you have only dreamed of, and find greater happiness overall.

Practice applying your thought controls to focus on the positive in any given situation rather than the negative. Negative thoughts are a product of fear for an outcome that you don't feel will be in your favor. In conquering the fear you will have conquered half of the battle that negative effects of stress and emotions can inflict in your life. If you relax your mind and work diligently to remove the negative thinking from your life, you will be removing much of the stress in your life that you are unknowingly placing upon yourself. With every negative thought that you have, stop yourself and look at the contrasting positive side. After practicing positive thinking, you will start seeing the positive before ever contemplating any negative thoughts or judgments.

Have you ever wanted to be more like someone else that you have met? Maybe you want to be more outgoing, more confident, more compassionate, or more spontaneous? Nobody will be perfect but we can sure improve a great number of our characteristics. (Williamson, 1992, 29) "When Michelangelo was asked how he created a piece of sculpture, he answered that the statue already existed within the marble. So it is with you. The perfect you isn't something you need to create, because God already created it." In other word's everything that you need is inside of you and you just have to chip off all of the built up fear and negativity that you have let accumulate over the years.

When you start your baby steps to self improvement, choose one area that you would like to change in your work environment and one area you would like to improve in your home life. Let's say at work you may want to feel more comfortable complimenting others. First baby step - one time per workday you will give a co-worker a positive compliment on any given topic. At home maybe you would like to be able to better communicate with your partner or communicate more than you do. First baby step - each day when you and your partner meet at home, you commit to stop what you are doing and ask, "How did your day go today?" then listen and share stories before returning to the tasks at hand.

If you have suffered from mental abuse that left you experiencing difficulties of accepting touch as a positive exchange of affection, start with baby steps such as accepting a hug of affection without pulling away. If you are fearful of social settings, then find a person least threatening in your eyes and approach them to say hello or ask them something about themselves. People love to talk about themselves they have a lot that they would enjoy sharing with others. This will start a conversation rolling and your tension will begin to fade.

Bear in mind that it is up to you to pick yourself up and brush yourself off, challenge yourself. You are a strong individual otherwise you wouldn't even be contemplating change. You can change any aspect of your life that you desire with focus and baby steps but nothing will happen overnight so don't get discouraged, recognize your accomplishments at every stage and once you defeat one fear select the next one that you would like to diminish.

If you need to take a break and take a step back, then do so but don't forget the world is still waiting for you on the other side, always stay committed to moving forward. There is a life waiting for you to live it, find happiness, and learn your passion. Listen with your heart to those small voices you will learn to recognize. Above all, never give up your journey. Relaxation and taking time for yourself will be a very important priority in your life. This is where you will gather strength and reenergize your spirit. Be sure you always make the time to be alone with your thoughts.

> *When you have pushed as hard as you can … push harder.*
> *When you have tried as hard as you can … try harder.*
> *When you have reached as high as you can … reach higher*

CHAPTER 8
RELAXATION TECHNIQUES

Understand that any disturbing or frustrating moment in time is not your whole life but a mere fragment of a day. Becoming stressed is not going to resolve any issue. Maintain your calming thoughts and know that the significance of this stressful minute is not important in relation to the rest of your life.

Below are some general stress relievers that create positive ways to escape from stress, followed by many techniques and exercises for you to choose from, to find relaxation. By implementing any of these ideas, you can create many good triggers that alert your body and mind that it is time to relax.

Keep in mind that by participating in relaxation exercises, you are maintaining your bodies balance by giving the mind a chance to rejuvenate. While giving your mind this break it signals your body to slow down and the tense muscles to loosen up returning your body to a healthy balance.

Creating balance with relaxation exercises can help you through any part of a given day. Relaxation is a contributor to life satisfaction, quality of life, health and wellness. It is essential to the longevity of human beings, especially because it helps to counteract stress.

GENERAL STRESS RELIEVERS

- If you live by a beach make a special trip so that you can take an extended walk along the sand and listen to the ocean waves. If there Is not a beach nearby, any area that has quiet surroundings will have the same effect. Your choice should be a place that offers peace and quiet. This let's our minds imagine that we have left the rest of the world behind and there is a break with no worries or stress.
- Listen to music, sounds of nature, even a constant hum of a fan for relaxation. Purchase sounds of your choice from a large array of compact disc's and carry a disk player with you so that you are prepared to escape to another world at any given time in your day. There are relaxation CD's that contain the sounds of ocean waves, nature, piano, or soothing music. Keeping soothing sounds around you lets your mind slow down from the day's activities and gives you a calm and serene feeling of peace.
- The use of Aromatherapy candles, potpourri, incense, and diffusers can help you relax and are great to use during meditation periods. Lavender and chamomile scents neutralize feelings of stress and

anxiety. These oils bring about a feeling of sedation, which is a calm and tranquil sense of being. Bergamot and Geranium produce a mild fragrance that soothes and relieves tensions throughout the mind and body. You can also find potpourri in many different colors which makes it easy to work in with any décor in any room, keep this fresh by adding a couple drops of oil once a week. Incense and incense holders are found in abundance and diffusers are currently one of the most 'hottest' sellers on the market.

- Significant others can save you a bundle when it comes to massage if they are willing to participate. When someone is placing pressure on your body, as they rub you can feel all of the tension melt away and your body grow heavier and heavier. Of course, you'll have to reciprocate the favor. There are also specialists in reflexology that can work on pressure points that are located in your hands and feet that release tension throughout the body.

- Hot cocoa to the rescue! Sometimes you just want to curl up in a chair wearing comfortable clothing and read a book. Books are a good escape from reality and you can get so totally engrossed that your thoughts don't drift in any other direction other than the direction of the book. This is a perfect time to make a cup of warm tea or hot chocolate to give you that extra treat.

- Daydreaming is a sample of meditation. The power of memories can be seen in the ability for a single unexpected scent in the air to invoke a past experience and bring back the associated thoughts from that place in time. This memory transports you as if you inadvertently stepped into a time capsule.

- Our minds memories give us the building blocks to plan, predict, dream, fantasize and define who we are in this vast universe. We all use the past to build our future by stringing together bits and pieces of knowledge that we gather as we grow. We utilize the power of positive memories to make a nest, our own haven of happiness that encircles us. In our travels we pick up souvenirs that are placed ritualistically within our surroundings to bring back happy moments in time, moments we never want out of reach. The best thing about memories is that you can always reflect back to a place in time you enjoyed and relive this time through your minds eye over and over again.

- We control all of our reactions by the thoughts we entertain in our minds. Every moment of every day is part of your life, yet so many times we rush through our days to get to the other end and the middle is nothing but a blur of activities. We need to introduce a thought process that reminds us to enjoy the moments.

Place a small sticker or picture of a rose (or some other reminder), randomly in areas that you spend large increments of time throughout the day, use this as a reminder to stop and absorb the moment, maybe take a five minute break, remind yourself to smile and take some deep breaths to relax. Train your body to slow down and smell the roses.

- Don't do today what can be put off until tomorrow. No, I don't mean procrastinate, just remember that not everything has to be completed by the end of this day, that's what tomorrows are for. Don't strap yourself into so many obligations or goals in one day that you must rush through your day just to get everything accomplished.

Relaxation Techniques and Exercises

There are many techniques and exercises that you can do on your own to promote relaxation. Below are exercises with examples on implementation and therapies that are very rewarding in reducing stress.

Breathing Relaxation Exercises
Meditation
Gaining Empowerment
Visualization Relaxation
Guided Imagery Meditation
Acupuncture
Reflexology
Biofeedback
Progressive Muscle Relaxation
Yoga
Chakras
Aromatherapy
Massage
Eye Relaxation
Home or Spa Facial
Physical Fitness
Expressive Therapies
Music Therapy
Writing Therapy
Art Therapy
Hypnosis
Hobbies
Create Your Environment

BREATHING RELAXATION EXERCISES

Breathing exercises are the simplest, quickest, most convenient, and one of the most effective techniques that you can use any time and any place where you encounter stress or anxiety. Follow these directions for top results.

Practice this technique while taking some time to relax at home, so you will be easily able to get these same results no matter where you are. It is a matter of first recognizing your body and mind are entering a stress mode then place your focus on your breathing taking deep breaths to increase your oxygen flow. When our blood vessels are narrow, less oxygen enters our cells. With practice, deep breathing will allow us to open the vessels and increase this oxygen flow. This is why breathing relaxation needs to be a priority in stress reduction.

If you dabble in aromatherapy it would be beneficial to first fill the room with a relaxing aroma. Sit in an upright position while administering this breathing technique, maintain proper posture, or lie comfortably, with your head slightly elevated a few inches from the floor. We rarely use the full functioning capabilities of our lungs. We tend to take shallow breaths that only utilize the uppermost areas of our lungs. These positions are two ways to support your body so that you have the full ability to fill your lungs completely.

Close your eyes. Closing your eyes will help you to block any visual distractions. The object is to focus all of your attention on the present moment and your breathing. Hands should be resting on each side of you and your legs should not be crossed. This allows open blood flow and the ability to feel each part of your body relax.

As you might observe a willow tree gently blowing in the breeze back and forth, easy and steady, relaxing and tranquil – this is your breathing in and out, slow and soothing. As we take in deep breaths, we exercise our lungs, building them toward optimum performance. The lungs become more proficient at the exchange of carbon dioxide and oxygen. This stress breathing technique may seem easy, but the results are effective and necessary to activate the stress-release mechanisms.

- Sit or lie comfortably.

- Close your eyes.
- Let your muscles relax and feel your body become heavy.
- Start your deep breaths as you attempt to fill your entire lungs with air.
- Breathe through your nose, breathing in slowly and deeply, keeping the focus on your diaphragm, and then release the air just as slowly.
- With each breath, your body gets heavier.
- Focus on the rise and the fall of your diaphragm as you breathe in and then breathe out.

Do this a couple dozen times, but there is no need to count—focus on your breathing.

If you fall asleep, don't worry—you'll wake up feeling relaxed, refreshed and back in control of your life. If your mind wanders from your breathing to what you had for lunch or what's on your list of tasks to complete tomorrow, just slowly push that thought aside and return your focus to your breathing.

When you want to end, merely allow your thoughts to enter and slowly bring yourself back to the moment.

Don't allow yourself to get frustrated when other thoughts intrude in your space, they will continue to arise, and you will simply need to push them aside and regain control of your focus. Continue to do this for as long as you are comfortable and can maintain focus.

Breathing relaxation techniques are used in many ways to deal with stress for many aliments to promote body and mind relaxation. By learning this technique you will become better equipped with ways to deal with stress when your body is prompted. When you are experiencing symptoms of stress one of the first warning signs that you may notice is that your breaths remain shallow but come more rapidly. After you actually practice breathing exercises for a few days, you'll become more aware of the way that you breathe and therefore recognize when stress is sneaking up on you. When you become aware that your breathing has quickened, begin to relax your body by using your breathing exercise. You will be prepared to quickly counteract the attack.

There is a 2 minute stress relief exercise to come, called the *quick fix meditation* that will give you step by step directions and a standard visualization to work with, as you practice breathing relaxation.

Even if you are busy during the day, once you become conscious of your breathing, you can remind yourself to take a deep breath to fill your lungs. Practicing your deep breathing is a great technique that queues your body to relax. Practice this exercise whenever time permits.

MEDITATION

Meditation is one of the exercises that take 5-10 minutes out of your day and is easily done at work or at home. The object of meditation is to make your mind a blank slate and clear all those congested thoughts, then your mind is able to view situations from new perspectives.

Many Individuals view this technique in a different light. It truly depends on your experience and in-depth training of the subject matter. For the purpose of creating balance in your life it is very useful. This form of relaxation allows you to give your mind the needed break in thoughts, so that you can quiet your mind and feel revitalized anywhere within two to twenty minutes.

(Carolyn Chambers, 2006, 149-150) "If you're an artistic person, you might do well with flame meditation. Light a candle in a darkened room. Sit a foot away from the candle and stare at it. Blow it out, and with your eyes closed, let the image of the candle come into your mind."

The benefit of meditation is that it allows you that break to acknowledge that anxiety is not permanent, that it passes into and out of your body without leaving a trace. When you focus on meditative thoughts, the extreme highs and lows of your emotional response to life will disappear and you will be transported to a more calming mental state.

There is not a specific encounter you are supposed to have, depending on your state of mind you will have a variety of outcomes. When positioning yourself, try to avoid lying on your bed. The floor, preferably with carpet, and a small pillow to prop under your head will be more effective. Many times people lie in bed at night and rehash their day's activities or plan tomorrow's projects and errands. If you place yourself in this situation, your mind will tend to wander more than usual and it will be hard to wipe your mind free of thoughts.

Revert to your breathing techniques, placing your focus on the rise and fall of your chest as your lungs fill with air and then slowly exhale feeling your mind relax. If you have a hard time clearing your thoughts to make your mind a blank slate, maintain positive thinking. Discouragement will only feed the negativity that we are trying to exclude from our lives. Next is a quick fix that incorporates a brief visualization that may assist you. You may also want to try some various yoga practices.

Practicing this short exercise is a great way to break away from the days activities to deal with stress. Try this meditation to calm and rejuvenate you within minutes. If you are in an area where you can use a CD, preferably ocean sounds, this is a great plus.

Quick Fix Meditation

Sit comfortably and relax.
Let your eyelids drop to a relaxed position or close your eyes.
Take deep breaths, slow breaths. You need to feel your heartbeat start to slow.
Focus on your breathing.
Temporarily erase all of those thoughts that are cluttering your mind. Keep focusing on your breathing until you start to feel calm and relaxed.
Now, picture the ocean, with its waves rolling in and breaking at the shoreline, then rushing up the beach over the sand, then being swept back into the sea. Hold this visualization in your mind's eye for a few minutes as you watch the waves rush up onto the beach and retreat back to the ocean.
Now shift your focus to the waves offshore.
Keep seeing them reduce in size until you visualize a smooth surface of water. Picture small ripples appearing over the surface and the sun as a soothing reflection off the water.
Hold this visual. Feel the sense of quiet and calm. Once you feel relaxed, bring yourself back to focus on your breathing. Breathe a few slow, deep breaths, exhaling just as slowly.
Open your eyes and return to the place that you're resting, and then return your thoughts to the present issues and tasks.

Use this quick fix as often as you can during the day to relax and keep your thoughts on a positive track. Remember, by relaxing your mind, your body will follow suit and you will have a much more successful and happy day.

Vibratory Stress Relief

If you have a problem maintaining focus and can't seem to stop the racing thoughts in your head you may want to try using a mantra to begin your meditation until you can clear your thoughts and gain focus.

This is a word or a phrase that you repeat over and over as you center your thoughts on your breathing. You can also choose to use a simple vibratory sound. One of the most common vibratory sounds is aumm.

This mantra is more effective when chanted aloud in a low hum. Words such as "I am free and at peace" or any number of personal statements may be more effective as you repeat them silently over and over again as a slow, soothing thought. Let the mantra drift and fade within your thoughts. If your thoughts get misrouted, simply return your focus to your breathing and start to repeat your selected mantra again.

GAINING EMPOWERMENT

Try this meditation on gaining empowerment to practice relaxation and regenerate your power from within.

Sit or lie in a relaxed position.
Close your eyes and focus on your breathing.
Feel each part of your body as it relaxes and grows heavy.
Now focus on the darkness.
Keep breathing, slowly and deeply, while maintaining your relaxed state of body and mind.
Visualize the sun in the distance. It's a bright yellow and white light but not distressing on your eyes.
As you relax, your body begins to feel very light and then begins to lift from your position and float above you. You are still keeping your focus on the sun.
You begin to drift slowly towards the light. You bathe in the warmth that radiates from its surface.
As you continue to glide closer and closer, the heat never intensifies but the warmth remains like a soft blanket wrapped around you on a chilly night.
The sun continues to grow larger and larger as you get closer.
The light is all that is in sight, and you are drifting into it.
The yellow white light is encircling your being, caressing your soul, and you are becoming one with the brilliant light and the warmth.
All the powers of life are connected to you right now. The light is recharging your strength and the warmth is renewing your powers of control.
You can stay there as long as you like and take comfort in your safe place.
When you would like to return you will begin to drift out of the light, and now you are no longer part of the light but can see the definition of the shape of the sun.
You continue to focus on the calm feelings and the relaxed body.
Focus on the sun as you drift further and further away.
You float over your body and gently re-enter your earthly shape.
As you lay there you feel comfortable, peaceful, and stress free.
Open your eyes and become conscious of the tranquil state of relaxation your body possesses.

Exit your meditation slowly and return to the challenges of the day with the knowledge that you have renewed strength and control.

VISUALIZATION RELAXATION

By using visualization relaxation and connecting it with emotion, individuals are able to heal from harmful past experiences, if they are ill they are able to seek relief by escaping to a pleasant, peaceful, happy setting or if they live with overwhelming fears they can, with baby steps, learn to overcome these fears. Today, many hospitals have some form of visualization therapy to help patients recover from serious illnesses or injuries.

Visualization is another word for imagery or guided imagery. These techniques all work with the same concept of connecting your visions to your emotions. (Jacobson, 1976, 251) "Tests indicate that when you imagine or recall or reflect about anything, you tense muscles somewhere, as if you were actually looking or speaking or doing something, but to a much slighter degree."

This is a quick sample of visualization. If I were to ask you how many chairs you have in your home you would look through your minds eye using visualization to scan each room counting the chairs, as you scan each room you are seeing more than the chairs you are looking at the room.

Sit or lie in a relaxed position, close your eyes and focus on your deep-breathing technique. Feel each part of your body as it relaxes and grows heavy. Take your time until you feel relaxed. (Bradshaw, 1988, [a] 176) "The most effective visualizations occur while your brain is producing alpha waves. Alpha waves result from complete relaxation."

The visualization below would allow someone who could not recover from childhood mental abuse to find relief in this exercise, after using it many times there will come a time that those hurtful memories will be accepted and placed in the past where they belong. For this visualization I liked the name 'The child within' because that's who we will be visiting on this mental escape from reality.

The Child Within

To start your visualization close your eyes and focus on the darkness behind your eyelids but keep your eyes relaxed.

Keep breathing, slowly and deeply, while maintaining a relaxed state of body and mind.

Into this darkness slowly visualize a garden coming to life. Notice the colors surrounding you. You see bright green leafy trees and flowers of every color, scattered throughout the nearby tall grass.

There is a path of stones leading the way in front of you and you follow the path. As you continue to leisurely follow the path, you watch the grass and the trees as they sway with the soft, gentle breeze. It's quiet, but you hear birds chirping in the distance.

Walk slowly and take in the beauty around you.

You look ahead and see a unique wooden door with ivy cascading over its entranceway. You are focused only on the door as you approach.

You open the door to the sight of a bright light and a staircase made of brilliant white gold.

You begin to climb the stairs and at the first level you notice a bag. On this bag is the word "worries," so you take all your worries and you place them into the bag. You don't hold back any of them—there is no need for them here.

You continue to the next level and you see a bag marked "fears," so you take all your fears and you place them into the bag. You are feeling so much lighter now, so relaxed.

You continue on your journey and on the next level you see a bag marked "doubts and insecurities," so you take all your doubts and insecurities and you place them into the bag.

Life feels so uncomplicated now that the bags are full, and you feel weightless.

As you are standing there on this landing you hear the whimpering of a small voice.

As you resume walking up the steps the whimpering becomes more distinct.

You take the last few steps and turn on the landing as you see a small body huddled in the corner and a small face with tears streaming down.

As you kneel down and inquire as to why the child is unhappy, you look into the child's eyes, and at that moment you understand that you are the child that you are reaching out to comfort.

You sit and listen as the child shares their sadness, you comfort them and offer your assurance that everything will turn out just fine; there is no longer a need to worry or suffer.

Through further conversation, the child begins to feel safe with you and eventually can let go of the fear and unhappiness to go with you now and become one.

You take the child's hand and walk to the next level, where you meet a young adult who is standing on the landing looking so lost, lonely, and sad.

Again you realize that this is another extension of you.

You sit down and begin to talk.

They tell you of their heartache, their wishes, and their dreams.

You are understanding and soothe their troubled heart, explaining to them that anything they have done in their life and anything they have experienced is not important now—everything is all right, you are healthy and you have found your way in life.

You know that any decision they made or any decisions made by those around them were made based on their knowledge, strengths, and fears at that stage of their life.

Things might have been different if the circumstances had been different, but you assure them that everything will work out for them.

You share with them that when they grow, there will always be many paths to choose from, but you do the best you can at that time and then you move forward.

You promise that they will see happier days and there will come a day when they will be triumphant, proud, and strong.

They smile, and you continue to share your thoughts about their past experiences.

Stay and visit as long as you like, and when its time to leave, return through the garden and slowly come back to the place you are resting.

(Bradshaw, 1988, [a] 142) "It is important to know that the need to find the Inner Child is part of every human being's journey towards wholeness. No one had a perfect childhood. Everyone bears the unresolved unconscious issues of his family history. You cannot go forward with fear and hurt in your heart and be happy." It's time to let go and enjoy the time you have left in this world and collect all of the happiness that has escaped you over the years.

GUIDED IMAGERY MEDITATION

Guided imagery meditation is a form of mind control that can allow a person to retreat from his/her surroundings and gain control over their thought process. This may be to deal with a stressful situation, to modify their own behavior or reaction to a situation, to create focus in attaining certain goals they wish to achieve, or simply for relaxation.

Our thoughts create pictures in our minds. If you are thinking about a vacation you have taken, you can see sights through your mind's eye when you think these thoughts. Guided imagery meditation takes the power of our mind and directs this energy to attain certain results. This form of mind control is used for physical benefits such as with stress reduction and its effects on the body, to psychological benefits such as calming a racing mind, enhance relaxation, or modify a person's perception.

It is best to assume a meditative position. Sit or lay with your arms to your sides and your legs uncrossed. Start by relaxing your mind and body with your breathing technique. Focus on and relax each body part; head, eyes, mouth, neck, arms, hands, shoulders, diaphragm, belly, hips, legs, and feet. Once your body is relaxed you will start your guided imagery meditation that you choose to use, one of your own or there are many CD's available for your purchase that allow you to focus on and listen to the voice as you are guided.

Let's say that your body is relaxed from your breathing technique and you have an image in your mind of you walking on soft white sand in front of a large body of water as it rolls into shore to cover your feet with a cool and refreshing sensation, a soft breeze brushes across your body, through your hair and on your face.

See the colors that you are viewing. You feel the warm rays of the sun on your skin as you are watching the birds scurrying in front of your steps, you can hear the water and some seagulls as they fly over head. You are there, you can look behind you and see your footprints left in the sand. You walk as long as you want and maybe collect some beautiful seashells along the way.

This special place that you have escaped to has an effect on your body as you walk the beach. Your mind is focused, your heartbeat has slowed, your breathing is relaxed, you feel the tranquility of the moments. In turn, your rising blood pressure can be lowered, pain sensations can be dulled, immune system regulated, adrenaline hormones and stress reactions reversed, and stress levels stabilize.

You can use these techniques in guided imagery meditation to modify your own behavior by changing your perception of a given situation and how you react to that situation by focusing on the desired results you would like to see. You can create focus in attaining certain goals in your career and visualize how you would like to perceive yourself in comparison to someone in the field that you look up to and value their demeanor and problem solving skills.

For example; if you wanted to meditate on something pertaining to what you want in the future, let's say, a fulfilling career in the field, holding the position that you desire. Your meditations may be to look at where you are now and what steps you want to take to reach your goals and then focus on where you are five years from now. "What are you doing?" "Where do you see yourself?" "What are you like as a person?" These practices help you to attain these goals by reinforcing your desires and the steps you need to focus on to get where you would like to be.

The positive uses of guided imagery meditation are endless, you can use this to assist with, phobias, lessen panic attacks, lower blood pressure, gain self confidence, help with feelings of depression, use for attaining life goals, grief therapy, reducing headache pain, finding your purpose in life, simple relaxation, problems with sleep disorders, spiritual enhancement, weight reduction, and virtually any specific condition or physical symptom. The use of self hypnotic tapes along with guided imagery are very helpful in stimulating deep relaxation, while working in any self improvement area that you choose to focus on. Tapes cover almost any type of behavior modification that you may be looking for. (Self hypnotism will follow.)

Susan J. Del Gatto

Acupuncture

In traditional Chinese medicine, it is believed that health is a result of the harmonious balance between the complementary extremes, yin and yang, and the life force known as qi or chi. Qi which has also been described as "vital energy" of the body. This energy flows through channels or pathways throughout the body and it is believed that ill health and disease may result from an imbalance or blockage of these forces.

There are twelve key pathways in the body that run vertically, bilaterally, and symmetrically. Each pathway is associated to points across the body which affects a particular organ or other body part.

(Bourne, 2001, 43) "In acupuncture treatment, the acupuncturist inserts thin needles at specific points of the body. Most people feel only a slight prick or no pain at all from the procedure. Typically the needles are left in place for twenty or thirty minutes, after which it's common to feel very relaxed and rejuvenated. Repeated treatments (twice a week for a few weeks) are often needed to correct an ailment such as migraine headaches, allergies, or back pain."

Prior to the acupuncturist positioning the needles you will be examined and questions asked to form an assessment of your needs and current condition. You will be asked to recline in a chair or lay down so that your body will be relaxed while the treatment is being administered. Once the needles are inserted they may be moved gently to promote stimulation.

The traditional Chinese theory behind acupuncture as medical treatment is very different from that of Western medicine. Modern western concepts use a more scientific approach in definition. In these terms it may be easier to comprehend that the nerves, muscles and connective tissue of the body are stimulated by way of needles releasing endorphins and increasing blood flow.

(National Acupuncture and Oriental Medicine Alliance) "Acupuncture has been cited by the World Health Organization to treat over forty-three conditions including allergies, asthma, back pain, carpal tunnel, colds and flu, constipation, depression, gynecological disorders, headache, heart problems, infertility, insomnia, pre-menstrual syndrome, sciatica, sports injuries, tendonitis and stress."

Check with your family physician or local hospital for a qualified acupuncturist in your area.

REFLEXOLOGY

Reflexology as we know it today, stemmed from the early works of William H. Fitzgerald, M.D. who founded zone therapy. Eunice D. Ingham, who was a physical therapist during this timeframe, took a great interest in this therapy and began to apply this concept to a foot reflex therapy she started developing in the early 1930's. Eunice spent the remainder of her life supporting and teaching her knowledge of reflexology.

The Ingham Method of reflexology has deciphered the locations of the nerves in the hands and feet, called reflex areas and associated them through years of research and documentation to a corresponding part of the body, gland, or organ that is directly stimulated when pressure is applied through massage on a particular nerve ending.

This is as similar belief as with acupuncture in that Reflexologists believe that the body contains an energy field, invisible life force, or Qi (chi), the blockage of which can prevent healing. A reflexology chart or map is usually found displayed in the doctor's office and this will illustrate to you the "reflex zones" worked by reflexologists on the soles of the feet. Similar maps exist for the position of the reflexes on the hands.

It is thought that this type of relaxation therapy when administered by a knowledgeable reflexologist may be able to reduce pain, swelling, and tension in the inner body through massaging the correlating nerves that communicate to this body part, from the feet or the hands. The therapist will use pressure to squeeze, stretch, and massage the affected area along with the entire foot or hand and release the built up tension that in turn interrupts the stress signal and resets the balance within the body. It is best if the patient remains quiet and focused on the relaxation of the body and the pressure being applied.

Reflexology of the hands is one of the easiest procedures to apply since you can apply this to yourself and you can apply this in essentially any setting whether you are at work, home, on a bus, in a movie theater, wherever and whenever the mood strikes you. It is best to obtain a book that illustrates movement direction and many techniques that work on the entire hand including the fingers, since pictures are more easily understood and in this case are definitely worth a thousand words.

(Kunz, 2006, 24) "The hands are particularly convenient for reflexology work. Whether you are applying reflexology to yourself or another, it is simple to reach out for a hand and apply reflexology technique. One of the clearest advantages of hand reflexology is the ease it offers of playing an active role in reducing stress levels."

You can learn techniques that may be worked on your hands by using a golf ball, a rubber stress ball, or a finger roller and apply the rolling motion along with pressure and a stretching motion on certain reflex areas. There are also foot rollers that you can use by laying them on the floor and resting your foot over the roller making a forward and then a backward motion with your foot to create the massage affect, this will also stimulate your reflex areas. These items such as mentioned above are small and can be carried with you, placed in your car, or carried in your purse.

BIOFEEDBACK

Wouldn't it be great to be able to communicate with your body? To tell it to sleep on demand, to remove pain when you ask or to know what it is that it needs? Biofeedback essentially does this. It teaches you to recognize what your body is saying and thus be able to give it what it is asking for.

Our bodies have a positive or negative reaction to anything we ask them to do. Biofeedback is what can help us decipher what the body needs from us to complete the task we are requesting. Our body may tense just before walking on a stage to do a presentation this may be a reaction of some fearful thought that has come into our mind. Our body is trying to tell us many things a day as it gives us physical clues such as being tired, fatigued, have constipation, diarrhea, and headaches, just as it gives us mental clues when we are feeling irritable, restless, impatient, depressed, confused, angry, or moody.

We have grown to understand some of our body's simpler communications with us, such as when our bodies begin to shiver and get goose bumps, we know we are cold and we can recognize when we are having a feeling in the stomach which we call hunger pangs, that we are hungry. The more we understand the sensations that our body is making us aware of, the closer we get to becoming one with our bodies and the more balance we integrate in our life.

This type of feedback takes time to become skilled at and a therapist trained in biofeedback must assist you in making this progress. This wouldn't replace a physician or medications in all instances but it would help in a number of other ways.

If you are unable to sleep for example your therapist may monitor your brain wave activity as you attempt to fall asleep and be able to guide you into being aware of how your body and mind are reacting to your request. They will continue to test your brainwave pattern in different scenarios, until you learn what it is that will alter your brainwave activity and give you the desired results. Your body and mind may be telling you that they can't shut down, so in this case using a number of relaxation techniques, and monitoring your body's response, it can be discovered what your body and mind respond to. Then when you perform this action, these brainwave patterns will be altered to permit sleep to come. Once you find the key and relate the feelings from your body to your mind you can notice how your body is reacting and understand what is going on inside to correct the problem.

Take another example of headaches. You may find that during a headache, you can manipulate your body in some way to trigger the relaxation needed to assist your body and diminish the headache. Maybe you will discover that particular thoughts and experiences bring on these headaches and uncover a painful experience that you need to deal with to release you from these thoughts.

Biofeedback will measure physiological functions that under normal circumstances you would not be able to recognize. This is done by the means of using a device that measures your reactions by brainwave, sweat glands, and skin temperature or muscle tension. (Carolyn Chambers, 2006, 93) "Biofeedback instruments monitor your body via electrodes that detect internal changes and transform them into visual or auditory signal, such as sound, a flickering light, or readings on a meter. The knowledge of how your body is reacting to certain stimulation will allow you to self regulate by changing the amount of stimulation or eliminating a particular stimuli to become more in tune with your body."

Biofeedback can be very successful at teaching you to overcome pain or anxiety by connecting the feelings you experience in your body just before these active episodes then use these feelings to distinguish the warning signs. This can alert you to take certain action to circumvent the negative reactions that are occurring within your body. With biofeedback you learn how to alter your actions based on the communication you are receiving, simply from the sensations you are feeling.

This is another good tool to use if you have an anger problem. Between techniques of visualization and muscle tension feedback you could stimulate the feelings of anger and then learn how to obtain control by applying a technique, for instance adjusting your perception and changing your thought patterns thus reducing the stress that has brought on the attack.

Not all therapists practice biofeedback therapy, this takes specific training and equipment to master this procedure. Your personal physician, counselor or local medical facility should be able to give you good recommendations based on their knowledge of local practitioners.

Progressive Muscle Relaxation

Edmund Jacobson, M.D. was the force and knowledge behind the progressive muscle relaxation theory. His research and interest in this topic started in 1908 at Harvard University and continued throughout his lifetime until his death in 1983. Throughout the years his technique has been used by many physicians, to teach their patients the art of relaxation.

The general idea behind his theory is that a person is able to persuade their body to relax by tensing each muscle and focus on the tightness of the muscle, then totally relax the same muscle and recognize the difference in the feeling between the body parts being tense, versus being relaxed. A sample as to how a physician may use this is below.

Read the exercise through first then attempt to lay flat in a comfortable position or sit comfortably in a chair, do not cross your legs and lay your hands to the sides of your body. Feel the ambiance as your body relaxes through each stage, until ultimately you have reached total body relaxation. I would suggest closing the eyes to block out any visual distractions.

Let's start with your head and work our way down your body.

With your eyes closed, lift your forehead muscles to create tense wrinkles in your forehead, hold the position for approximately 10 seconds and then without making any effort, totally let that muscle relax and fall back to its original positioning. Notice the feeling of the relaxed forehead.

Next squeeze your eyes together as hard as you can and again hold for 10 seconds then immediately let go of the tension and let your eyes relax. Feel your eyes as they are when they are totally relaxed.

Wrinkle your nose, hold for the same amount of time and then relax in the same way as above.

Do the same for the following body parts.

Mouth/Lips - push out, hold
Jaw - open mouth as wide as you can, hold
Neck – lift your shoulders and squeeze
Shoulders – push them back, hold – push them forward, hold

Lower Back – tighten
Abdomen/Belly – tighten
Buttocks – tighten
Right leg – tighten
Left leg – tighten
Right foot – tighten
Left foot – tighten

When you have successfully completed this exercise and relaxed your total body, take the time to lay or sit still for a moment, absorbing the sensations of the relaxed body. Stay this way as long as you can or would like, maybe even splurge and take a nap.

YOGA

Yoga dates back before writings of history began. This practice is a Hindu philosophy that involves certain physical and mental disciplines, together with a withdrawal from the world and abstract meditation upon a spiritual principal or object.

(Castleman, 2000, 43) "Most of the research comes from India, where yoga is practiced in conjunction with both Western medicine and Ayurveda, India's traditional medicine. But American and European researchers have also put yoga under the microscope, publishing their findings in leading Western scientific journals. Their studies show that yoga can help with heart disease, high blood pressure, diabetes, asthma, and back pain."

The purpose is to achieve both physical and spiritual well-being. This activity allows the individual to bring closer or unite the soul and the cosmos through a state of self-realization. There are many different interpretations that are practiced, each being similar and with the same goals but some being more in depth or an expansion of their counterpart. Individuals themselves that practice this form of physical and spiritual relaxation are called Yoginis for the females and Yogis for the males.

With the practice of yoga, it is important to get to know the inside energy points of your body, these are called chakras. Chakra in Sanskrit means wheel. These wheels are the center of activity that receives life force energy. The Hatha Yoga is one of the more popular practices that use many different forms of physical poses, as well as breathing exercises and purification techniques, to calm the mind and allow for a positive flow of spiritual energy.

This is accomplished by exploring the inner structure of the body mind and spirit. When achieving a balance between the mind and the body the chakras are unblocked and open to send a positive energy flow throughout each chakra until an ultimate enlightenment is achieved.

Hatha is a Sanskrit word meaning sun and moon. This depicts the opposing forces or energies. This physical fitness ritual and meditation are extremely complementary to each other. After partaking in a yoga session your body is relaxed and you feel revitalized.

I have found it very beneficial to purchase tapes that visually show me poses that I can imitate, while listening to the instructors words. There are a number of yoga classes offered at many exercise facility's one of which may be in your area, check the local telephone directory under gyms and call to obtain their schedule.

CHAKRAS

Each chakra center is said to be linked to physiological functions, color, and other distinguishing characteristics. There are diverse models from traditional to modern of the chakra system within the human body. Each chakra works in relationship to each other. They spin and draw in this energy to keep the spiritual, mental, emotional, and physical health of the body in balance. If there are days that you feel energized while other days you feel fatigued, this may be that your chakras are imbalanced. Chakras are thought by some to have a relationship between the positions and functions of the chakras, and of the various glands and other organs of the body.

Traditional Chinese medicine also relies on a similar model of the human body as an energy system, except that it involves the circulation of qi energy. The qi energy connects the flow of energy from one chakra to the next.

The study of chakras will teach the seven principal chakras, which are said to reflect how the unified consciousness of humanity is divided to manage different aspects of earthly life. The top of your head (or crown) being concerned with pure consciousness and the bottom (or root) is concerned with matter.

Starting from the base of the spine upwards the chakras listed below, discuss each point with some of their associated physiological functions, color, and other distinguishing characteristics.

Root Chakra – The root is located at the base of the spine. This is associated with the color red and the word earth, as it is thought that it grounds us to our physical world and creates stability. This is also associated with security and survival. This would be the chakra that alerts the body with the fight or flight response that we relate with our reactions to stress.

Spleen Chakra – The spleen chakra point is located in the lower abdomen and associated with the color orange. This is also related with the word water, which is fluid and readily changing. The primary functions being creativity and sexual energy.

Solar Plexis – The solar plexis chakra is located at the mouth of the stomach and is associated with the color yellow and the word fire, which depicts a strong mix of will and intensity of spirit, feeling, and passion. This also has an influence over the emotions of joy and anger and said to be of energy, since it is correlated with the digestive system that converts the food that we eat to energy for the body.

Heart – The heart chakra is located in the center of the chest and is associated with the color green and the word air, which depicts the open space around and above the earth. The primary functions are love, wisdom, equilibrium, and compassion. This chakra is also related to the thymus organ in the body, which is unfavorably affected by stress.

Throat – The throat chakra is located in the body at the base of the throat and is associated with the color blue and the components of life and sound. This represents growth, expression, and communication, which is beneficial to balance with song, humming or conscious breathing.

Third Eye - The third eye chakra is located in the body on the forehead centered between the eyebrows and is associated with the color indigo and the components of time and light. This represents intuition, imagination, psychic abilities, and visualization.

Crown - The crown chakra is located in the body on the top of the head and is associated with the color violet and the components of space and thought. This is said to be the highest point, the point of enlightenment. This is associated with the higher realms, spiritual connection and union with God.

(Toy, 2002, 54) "Each of the Chakras relates to particular parts of the body, and an imbalance in the energy of a particular chakra may mean that the related areas may be more susceptible to illness and disease. If we understand the nature of the energy of each chakra, it may be possible to support physical healing by examining the emotional/mental/energy aspects of the corresponding chakra."

The study of chakras will aid you when you feel out of balance, to be able to recognize where your problem may lie. While practicing yoga and working with each chakra, your goal is to produce balance and bring harmony to your inner being. Imbalances may show outwardly, indicating to you a need to focus and bring back into balance a particular chakra. If you are experiencing heart problems then your focus should be on your heart chakra, anger – your solar plexis, emotional problems on your spleen, communication issues on your throat, and so on.

AROMATHERAPY

Aromatherapy healing is the use of a blend of extracted botanicals, using a variety of plant materials that are processed to develop concentrated oil. This concentrated oil is called essential oils. These oils affect the calmness of our minds, just as some herbs do when they are processed and ingested into our systems by swallowing a pill.

(Castleman, 2000, 299) "Lavender is an aromatherapy favorite for relaxation and insomnia. You can buy lavender essential oil in many health food stores and through mail-order catalogs." Essential oils are used in a variety of healing treatments. Parts of our brain can be triggered to obtain a desirable response as we ingest the plant by breathing the aroma released into the air. Different scents are said to alter moods, instill calmness, and promote healing. When suffering from stressful episodes, anxiety and/or depression, there are four aromatherapy essential oils that are rated high in relieving these aliments.

They are bergamot, geranium, lavender, and chamomile.

When you are feeling less than happy but not severely withdrawn in a depressive state of mind, the aromatherapy to use would be bergamot. Bergamot is extracted from fruit peel and creates an aroma that produces a mild fragrance that soothes and relieves tensions throughout the mind and body. Geranium is also known for relieving tension. Obtained from South Africa this oil is extracted from a perennial shrub, used commonly in perfumes due to the flowery aroma.

When using an aromatherapy diffuser the scent is carried on air particles that are inhaled and produce feelings of calm, contentment, and rest. This is perfect for a Sunday afternoon siesta. As more and more professionals use aromatherapy healing to reduce the effects of stress, our knowledge of these oils continues to expand and offer great relief for our day to day challenges.

If in doubt of mood altering affects of aromatherapy … stand up to the challenge. Have you ever out of the blue got a whiff of a scent that took you back in time to a place in the past? Maybe Grandma's house at a holiday gathering or Mom's linen's as you slid between the sheets? Thoughts are a direct result of emotions and the sense of smell can take you on a path of tranquil sensations.

Our senses are the most natural stress relief that we have but most people don't look within, they are too focused on searching for a miracle drug to make them feel good. Believe me, natural stress relief through our senses using aromatherapy healing is just as effective and much less expensive.

When in a depressive state of mind the strongest scents that neutralize these feelings of stress and anxiety lead to the scents of Lavender and chamomile. These oils bring about a feeling of sedation which is relaxing coupled with a calm serene sense of being.

Lavender may be the most popular of these perennial herbs because of its ability to mix so well with many other aromas. This then clears the way for a wide array of products of all kinds. You can find lavender in lotions, sprays, bath salts, spa massage oils, perfumes, sachets, and many other items. When being applied directly to the skin they should not be used in their concentrated or undiluted state.

The difference you see in the price of products is due to its purity level. This is the level of concentrated oil in the product you are purchasing. The essential oils are the most concentrated of oils and therefore, are the most expensive of aromatherapy products.

I prefer the method of aromatherapy healing, by use of essential oils distributed throughout the air by the use of an electric or reed diffuser. When unable to use this form of therapy then using the more subtle effect such as sachets, lotions, car diffusers, shampoo's and conditioners etc. allow the aroma to always be within close proximity to your sense of smell through the day to help maintain a more calm and relaxing demeanor.

This therapy can be beneficial by being both psychologically, as well as physically effective. Whether the oil is inhaled or penetrates through the skin the effects within the body's chemistry create a sense of balance and in turn produce feelings of harmony. There are many decorating tips that include aromatherapy products to help you create a haven of relaxation. These blends of oils have been used for many years throughout our history, with the practice of meditation. They are said to unite the mind and spirit with the body, creating a therapeutic and healing effect.

There are many products, such as eye masks made with lavender and flax seed, that are manufactured today that allow us to use the benefits of aromatherapy healing in our everyday active lifestyles. These products can be used in a work setting, a home setting and/or a meditation setting. The use of aromatherapy helps us instill calmness in our hectic lives and remain relaxed in our environment.

Although there may be positive uses for aromatherapy, this practice is not suggested if you are or may be pregnant.

MASSAGE

Massage with Aromatherapy, is a relaxing and healing treatment that can be done with your partner in a home setting. Massage is an effective way to relieve stress, anxiety, and tension. A massage using essential oils combines the balancing properties of the oils, with the relaxing and therapeutic benefits of touch. Essential oils have a powerful therapeutic affect that can delight the senses and lift the spirits.

(Stuart, 2007, 369) "Start releasing the underlying tension, use essential oils in what is called a massage blend. As the massage movements begin to work on the aching muscles at surface and deeper levels, the oils begin to be absorbed. In time they too get to work and start tackling the inner tension."

If you are stressed, out of balance, or simply wanting to lift your spirits and enjoy the fragrances of essential oils, massage therapy will show you how to unwind. There is nothing more relaxing or therapeutic than a deep massage. With stress escalating, massage is currently available everywhere from airports to workers' cubicles.

Sharing massage between you and your partner offers the pleasure to give and receive. This can bring special feelings of satisfaction, connection, and closeness with another. Even preparing for the experience can stir excitement, as you set the mood and select fragrant oils. This massage is most beneficial if you can drift off to sleep relaxed after the massage and wake up feeling refreshed and rejuvenated. Whatever the pleasure relax, de-stress, and most of all enjoy.

Spa Massage is used for a multitude of reasons – pain relief and reducing stress are two common reasons for most individuals to seek this treatment. Practice of manipulation of the soft body tissue has physical, functional, and therapeutic purposes and goals. Target tissues may include muscles, tendons, ligaments, skin, joints, or other connective tissue. The actual massage can be applied with hands, fingers, elbows, forearm, and feet among many other application techniques.

Different positions of massage are available, in a spa you are more apt to lie on a table, while at your place of employment or any other social setting they may offer a 15-20 minute stress reducing massage by sitting upright in a massage chair.

(Stuart, 2007, 100) "Our muscles give the body strength and movement. To work effectively, they need a good balance between movement, exercise, and relaxation. Holding the muscles in the same position for extended periods of time, such as when working on a computer terminal, makes them contract and shorten, impeding the circulation and flow of nutrients through the muscle fiber. This leads to muscle spasm and stiffness. Massage works effectively to reduce tightness in the muscles of the body that accumulates over time, especially when a person is under stress or has a sedentary lifestyle."

Theories behind what massage might do include, stimulating the release of endorphins and serotonin, improving sleep, decreasing muscle tension, increasing flexibility, and reducing blood pressure by increasing the blood flow, making the body relaxed and better able to function.

There is a long list of the types of massages that are available. One of the most prevalent spa massages is called the Swedish massage where they use long, flowing strokes performed with open hands and accommodated with oil, cream, or lotion applied to the skin to reduce friction. Other massage techniques use kneading movement with the whole palm or finger tips, using wringing, skin rolling, compression, and/or lifting.

The United States does require the massage profession to be licensed by having a certificate, diploma, or degree depending on the particular school and they must attend continuing education requirements to maintain this status.

Give yourself a gift of a spa massage treatment and feel the results of a relaxed, stress free body. Never forget to pamper yourself. Feet carry the weight of your body and are restricted in the shoes that you wear, which over time may cause the feet to become tired and sore, thus creating stress throughout the entire body.

Some easy techniques to reduce the tension in your feet would be to:

1. Roll a tennis ball under your foot. This is a great way to stretch the long tendon that runs along the planter surface of the foot from the heel to the ball of the foot.

2. Pour hot water into a basin with a cup of Epsom salts and eight drops of Lavender oil or use a spa treatment foot massage bath, soothing heat helps maintain the warm water temperature.

Eye Relaxation

Eye relaxation and/or eye therapy has had to become an integral part of a daily and weekly regimen for overall general eye health and relaxation. The main reasons for this alert to eye health stems from our vast expansion in computer use, as well as the substantial decay of the earth's protective ozone layer. Sun rays, stress, more work, less sleep, and fatigue can cause red puffy bloodshot eyes that need relief.

Squinting and straining the eye muscles to focus on the bright computer screens causes more stress on the eyes optic nerve. The more hours you spend pecking on the keyboard and watching a blinking curser the more stress you place on these nerves. There is also harmful substances called 'free radicals', these are unstable oxygen molecules that cause cell damage.

Most individuals believe running to the store or playing catch in the back yard are short term exposure to the suns rays and therefore cause no need to protect the eyes. This was a more accurate statement years ago but due to atmospheric changes, it has become more important to protect your eyes at all times. Exposing your eyes to ultra violet light damages the proteins within the lens of your eyes, these damaged proteins group together and ultimately result in the formation of cataracts. Your goal should be to filter 95-100% of the suns ultra violet rays.

(BNET Business Network) "Harvard Eye Associates Expert Warns Against Sun Damage to the Eyes – Expert ophthalmologist and eye plastic surgeon Dr. Jeffrey Jacobs of Harvard Eye Associates, based in Laguna Hills and San Clemente, cautions patients to limit and protect themselves from sun exposure when levels of UV radiation are particularly high – between 10:00 am and 4:00 pm Especially on overcast days, at high altitude or on reflective surfaces such as water and sand, UV rays are particularly damaging."

The following techniques will reduce daily stress and fatigue that may be the cause of tension headaches or the pressures of eye strain caused by over work, bright lights, and computers.

- To relax the optic nerve you will need to close your eyes and visualize looking at the inside of your eye lids. You will be seeing the color black if you do this correctly. Our mind can visualize different colors depending on our thoughts that lead our visualizations. The color black will allow the optic nerve to perform the least amount of activity. This relaxation technique is the most easiest to use while at work along with palming.

- The use of an eye mask is both calming and therapeutic. This also helps so that you don't have to focus so hard at holding your eyes closed, which will allow a more complete relaxation. Spa relaxation techniques include placing cool astringents on the eyes such as sliced cucumbers, chilled aquamarine stones, or cotton pads soaked in witch hazel. These are placed over your eyes while you are in a relaxed horizontal position. Another spa technique is to steep two chamomile tea bags in hot water then set them aside to cool, when they have cooled to lukewarm, place them on the eyelids. To eliminate all light, place an eye mask of lavender or chamomile over the tea bags and lay in a relaxed position for 10-20 minutes. After this treatment place a cool washcloth over your eyes for 1-2 minutes. This treatment will help your eyes fell fresh, awake and rejuvenated.

- Palming is an eye relaxation technique that offers your eyes a relaxing massage. To do this, interlock your fingers so that your palms are facing each other, now spread open your fingers and open your hands to view your palms. Place your crossed fingers on your forehead this will place your eyes in the palms of your hands. Without directly putting pressure on your eyelids move your hands in a circular motion. This will cause a relaxing pressure of massage around the perimeter of the eyes reducing eye tension.

HOME OR SPA FACIAL

Wipe your stress away with a facial ... a relaxing treat that has substantial benefits to making you feel good as well as look good. You may get a treatment at a spa anywhere from an average of $50.00 to $100.00 or if you prefer you can purchase skin treatments that you can perform at home at your own convenience.

Exfoliation involves the removal of the oldest dead skin cells along the skin's outermost surface. Exfoliation is involved in the process of a facial and during body treatments at spas. It is a process recommended to maintain healthy skin at least twice a week, with a daily regimen recommended during the winter months.

Facial moisturizers are complex mixtures for skin treatments containing chemical agents specially designed to make the external layers of the skin softer and more pliable, by increasing its hydration. The inexpensive brands of moisturizers may be less pure in their active ingredients leading to irritation of the skin along with a less potent formula leading to fewer positive effects. In comparison, you will note with the lower end brands that they do contain highly regarded ingredients but in lower concentrations which yield lower benefits to the skin.

When preparing for a facial, look for smaller packaging, subtle floral scents, essential oil mixtures from flowers and plants, plus high concentrations of vitamins and acids. The usual price ranges are between $30.00 and $70.00

A facial mask is a creamy mask applied to the face for hygiene effects To clean and smooth the face. It often contains minerals, vitamins and fruit extracts, such as cactus and cucumber, to give the nutrition to the skin of the face. There are different kinds of masks for different purposes; some are deep cleansing for cleaning the pores. The effect is revitalizing, rejuvenating, and refreshing. Facial masks are most commonly used by women but also used by men. Some masks are washed off with tepid water, while others are peeled off by hand. Duration for wearing a mask depends on type of mask, but can be 3 minutes to 30 minutes, and sometimes including the whole night.

A cleanser is a facial care product that is used to remove make-up, dead skin cells, oil, dirt, and other types of pollutants from the skin of the face.

This helps to unclog pores and prevent skin conditions such as acne. Many people use a cleanser one or more times a day as part of their skin care regimen, together with a toner and moisturizer. Using a cleanser to remove dirt is considered to be a better alternative to bar soap or another form of skin cleanser that are not specifically formulated for the face for the following reasons:

- Bar soap has a high pH (in the area of 9 to 10), and skin's natural pH is 5.5. This means that soap can change the balance present in the skin to favor the overgrowth of some types of bacteria, exacerbating acne. pH is a measure of the acidity or basicity of a solution.
- Bar cleansers in general, soap or not, have thickeners that allow them to assume a bar shape, this can clog pores, leading once again to acne.
- Using bar soap on the face can remove natural oils from the skin that form a barrier against water loss.

It is important to remember to always wash your face in lukewarm water, use a milky cleanser and a hydrating toner. Try not to leave the skin un-moisturized for too long after cleansing. It is imperative not to de-hydrate the skin. Cleanse, tone, and moisturize twice a day, once at night and once in the morning.

EXPRESSIVE THERAPIES

Expressive therapy is the intentional use of the creative arts as a form of therapy. This type of therapy works under the assumption that through the imagination and the various forms of creative expression, humans can heal. The three expressive therapies will be explained more at length in the following pages.

1. Music is a form of expressive therapy used and taught to be a mood stabilizer. It has the capabilities to increase your energy, instill relaxation, make you happy, make you sad, or make you reflective of past memories. We react both emotionally and physically.

    To understand this and feel this, pick out a CD that has fast dance music and one that has instrumental slow music, then listen to each one noting the feelings emotionally and physically that take place within yourself.

2. Writing is a form of expressive therapy that uses the act of writing and processing the written word as therapy. The act of writing allows the individual to form detailed thoughts and relay these thoughts to paper.

    The pain of speaking may be to unbearable for some individuals but in releasing the words to paper it can grant a form of relief as well as taking a necessary step towards acceptance in certain cases. Writing therapy can be kept private and used as a form of self awareness or it can be shared with a therapist or counselor.

3. Art is another popular form of expressive therapy. In this therapy with the use of a variety of materials individuals will draw, paint, sculpt or use photography to help cope with stressful issues, work through traumatic experiences, increase insight and cognitive abilities, as well as enjoy the life-affirming pleasures of the creative experience.

When used in the medical field these therapists are trained to recognize the non-verbal symbols and metaphors that are communicated within the creative process that individuals find difficult to put into words or expression.

MUSIC THERAPY

Music therapy is the manipulation of using music coupled with an individual's settings and circumstances to generate desired behaviors. Music is a mood stabilizer. It has the capabilities to increase your energy, instill relaxation, make you happy, make you sad, or make you reflective of past memories.

Music was discovered and developed since almost the beginning of time. It is composed and performed for many purposes, ranging from aesthetic pleasure, religious and/or ceremonial purposes amongst others. Over the many years and through the many cultures the use of different instruments has given rise to numerous forms of song and dance.

Sounds are strung together in such a way that they can calm the mind. Today it is more so an entertainment product for the market place. In an effort to encourage relaxation and reduce stress it has been found that certain soothing sounds can promote relaxation through mental stimulus. This stimulation can automatically trigger a visualization depicting a calm surrounding, such as a beach with ocean waves or a quiet wooded area with a trickling stream and chirping birds.

Music, when used as a therapy, has been found beneficial in unison with massage therapy, aromatherapy, and meditation relaxation. With the use of music and harmony the instruments and intermingling of notes at just the right pitch, can persuade the mind to use the rhythm of the music to control the breathing of an individual. This will determine the depth of relaxation a person will experience up to and including even inducing sleep.

Most individuals experience stress in a work or a home environment during the more active periods of their day. Although your mind needs to stay alert during these times and focused on completing your tasks, you can use the power of music therapy and your subconscious mind to your advantage. By placing the smooth rhythm of classical music in the background at a low volume, you can keep your breathing and heart rate at pace with the music and use these subliminal messages without interrupting the intensity of focus to your job duties.

There are many classical artists to select from but the top artists in this field will always remain with Mozart, Bach, and the more romantic classical sounds from Beethoven. If you are an individual who has listened to types of classical music before and the selection you were introduced to may not have been one to your liking, there is a special CD that was made just for you. Released in1994, it is called *Classical Music for People Who Hate Classical Music.*

WRITING THERAPY

Writing therapy gives you the time to decipher all of the thoughts and emotions that are attaching themselves to a particular subject. The primary key is time. This therapy lets you place your thoughts on paper and this then allows you to let go of the thoughts knowing that you can pick them up at a later time. In doing this you give yourself the needed time to relax the mind, which will help you to open up and entertain new ideas. This is also a great way to decrease the racing thoughts that keep you awake at night.

The most stressful life situations can turn into your best creative writing ideas. To understand this theory choose one of your top issues that is contributing to stress in your life and write this topic on a piece of paper. This action alone starts to generate thoughts.

When you start to think of this topic you will have many sub-topics form in your thoughts. This is what you start to write about. Notice the thoughts circling as you write looking for the next thought you want to place on the paper. These are your feelings coming to the surface as you write.

Now after you have written for some time, stop and read what you have wrote. You could have said all of this within minutes but would you have used the same thought process to be sure you covered all the topics that came to your mind? Between the thoughts and the paper we are given time to rotate all of our thoughts through a cycle that ensure we are coving each point we would like to make, while talking doesn't allow us the benefit of this time.

Try this – flip the papers over and as if speaking to another person, discus the topic you had previously written about. After you are done, look back to the paper and see what points of thought you had missed.

Writing therapy is private and it allows you to have something solid to reference rather than random and fleeting thoughts that come with no particular logic. This helps you to view the root problem, with a different perception and open your mind to new paths of resolve.

As we see, writing can help us to cope with any given situation attached to stress, as well as overcome issues of fear. Fear is the number one reason that individuals hold back from pursuing their dreams. There is no time to hold back, time escapes us far too quickly. This technique will guide you through your life with confidence, goals and a sense of direction.

ART THERAPY

There are progressive forms of art therapy from self help to professional guidance. This therapy is popular as a self-help therapy due to the meditative state, with focused concentration on one project. With centered focus an individual can relax the mind which in turn relaxes the body. This activity, as other expressive therapy's, is self rewarding twofold both in physical and mental wellness.

Art therapy can be done outside the home with groups such as taking a pottery class, art class, or quilting therapy class. Outside groups allow your mind to relax as you pull your focus from your immediate pressures, to group conversations and social interaction. This is a very favorable therapy for loneliness and problems of seclusion. If you find your life is overly active and you are racing from one task to the next than using art as a form of therapy in the privacy of your own home may be most suitable.

It's best but not necessary, to set aside a particular retreat space that will prevent interruptions and give you some quiet time. As you pour all of your concentration and focus into your project, it will give your mind the needed break in the activity that it needs to rejuvenate. You may also choose to use this quiet period to draw your focus to one particular subject matter that you may be having a problem with, while you are engrossed with working on your project. This can afford you the time needed to review possible solutions with their probable outcomes so that you can resolve an occurring dilemma you are facing.

If you would like to experiment with this therapy for relaxation and stress reduction but you don't have any ideas of interest to develop a project, review the list of hobbies that appear further in this book for any ideas that may peek your interest.

You may find art programs in a number of settings including:

- Hospitals
- Clinics
- Public and community agencies
- Wellness centers
- Educational institutions

- Private practices

The key to this therapy is to learn to relax and therefore, reduce stress.

HYPNOSIS

The Power of the Mind - we all need the positive self talk that hypnosis can deliver when we are feeling low, whether it's to motivate ourselves or develop a strong sense of worth, overcome some fears or negative emotions, ease pain or just to learn something new. Sometimes we get in a rut and can't use our imagination to see outside the box … another way of looking at a situation … a way to overcome a negative behavior or thought. Self-hypnosis (or auto suggestion) — in which a person hypnotizes himself or herself without the assistance of another person to serve as the hypnotist — is a staple of hypnotherapy-related self-help programs.

There are four states of the mind known as the beta state, this is when we are awake, the alpha state, this is when we are alert but relaxed, the theta state, this is our dream state of mind as we are falling into a deep sleep, and delta, which is our state of deep sleep. The alpha state is the state of mind we enter when we use hypnosis this keeps us alert to suggestion and our body and mind relaxed to accept the suggestion. To target your thoughts and make changes and improvements in your life, you have to focus on one thought pattern over and over again, until your mind accepts this thought process without you having to direct your mind to these focused thoughts.

(Streeter, 2004, 51) "It is often said by hypnotists that all hypnosis is really self-hypnosis. This means that the hypnotist's main role is to help subjects go into their own hypnotic trance, rather than to hypnotize them. It is we that go into the trance; the hypnotist simply helps us along the way."

The easiest way to train your mind through consistent thought patterns is a trained hypnotist recording that you can listen to, that is directed to the behavior that you want to change. You will find that positive thinking and self hypnosis are valuable tools to gain knowledge, success, and power in any area of your life that you are seeking to improve. Hypnosis gives you the availability to choose and focus on one given behavior you would like to change at a time.

There are hundreds of topics to help the self-hypnotist. Just a few of these can be topics such as:

Stay on a Diet	Overcome Smoking
Boost Self Esteem	Feel Good About Yourself
End Negative Thoughts	Self Sabotage
Overcome Stage Fright	How to Stop Worrying
Positive Thinking	Accepting Yourself
Self Confidence	Forgiving Others
Relief from Pain	Ease Anxiety Attacks
Increase Self Motivation	Anger Management
Lift Insomnia	Ease Depression

If you visit the Internet and search for 'self hypnosis downloads' you will find a wide array of choices that are available.

There is a common claim that no one can be hypnotized against their will. Some schools of thought hold that this procedure or treatment is a state of extreme concentration, where a person becomes oblivious to his or her surroundings while lost in thought. Often suggested as an example of self hypnosis is what might be called, highway hypnosis. This is when a driver suddenly finds themselves much further down the road without any memory of driving between point A and point B.

This procedure has also received publicity about its use in Forensics, Sports, Education, and physical therapy and rehabilitation. (Streeter, 2004, 76) "In 2000, researchers at Beth Israel Deaconess Medical Center in Boston found that hypnosis was able to reduce both surgical pain and surgery time, and improve safety. In a trail of 241 patients, it was discovered that patients that used self-hypnotic relaxation techniques during surgery generally needed less pain medication and left the operating room sooner. They also had more stable vital signs during the operation."

HOBBIES

Creating a hobby will initiate a program that you can count on to keep your stress at a minimum and introduce balance into your life on a regular basis. When your mind is entertaining a great number of thoughts at one time and then even more demands are placed on you that require your attention, you cannot possibly be effective. Just as exercise, nutrition, and sleep keep our bodies healthy, mind relaxation keeps us mentally healthy.

When our minds need to relax they have there own way of communicating that to us. Symptoms of stress such as confusion, fatigue, depression, anger, frustration and mood swings, will produce negative or unhealthy behavior. Some individuals use the method of taking a power nap during the day to rejuvenate their minds. If you're not one to nap then a leisure pursuit is a great alternative. You can work on a different choice of activity at your leisure, whether that's every day, a couple times a week, or once a week.

There is such a wide range of hobbies that you are almost guaranteed to find one that will be to your liking. Some individuals prefer a performing art, such as acting, juggling, magic, or dancing. Others prefer less active participation and more solitude, taking comfort and sometimes even gaining a profit with a creative hobby. Some examples could be woodworking, jewelry making, playing an instrument, software projects, artistic projects, creating models out of paper called paper craft, up to higher end projects, like building or restoring a car or building a computer from scratch. While some of these may just be for the enjoyment of the hobbyist, there has been instances where their projects have come into demand at the request of friends or passerby's when your work is seen by others who value your creativity. At this point it has the potential to become a small business.

To avoid getting tired of just one activity you may try a couple and alternate your choices such as joining a bowling league, but when you are not practicing bowling you might enjoy quilting or maybe you want to establish your own garden, but at night you find it relaxing to curl up in front of the television and crochet.

These lists cover hobbies from relaxing to active all of which are a means not only to reduce stress but also to create balance and harmony within your life.

Relaxing less physical activities:

Kite flying
Horse riding
Yoga
Astronomy
Amateur or Ham Radio Operator
Bird watching
Fishing
Camping
Website building
Beading
Jewelry making
Sewing
Knitting
Cross-stitch
Embroidery
Quilting
Crochet
Srcapbooking
Collage building

Choices that take up a bit of space but are great ideas are:

Glass blowing
Candle making
Leather crafting
Soap making
Stained glass art

Social inclusions that may also be considered:

Creating a family or friend game night; there are multiple board games plus many choices of card games available.

Model building offers many choices:

Cars
Aircrafts

Ships

Rockets

Trains (there is also train tracks and cities you can develop in miniature style.)

For shopping and collecting, some more expensive than others:

Antiquing

Collecting artworks

Crystals

Minerals

Seashells or rocks

Bottles

Coins

Stamps

Comic books

More artistic:

Painting

Drawing

Writing

Calligraphy

Pottery

Woodworking or carving

Playing an instrument

Somewhat active to very active:

Caving

Hunting

Hiking

Gardening

Swimming

Rafting

Sailing

Water skiing

Canoeing

Scuba diving

Surfing

Weight lifting

Rock climbing

Snow skiing

Aerobics
Dancing
Jogging
Roller skating
Ice skating
Tennis
Basketball
Bowling
Softball
Golf
Racquetball
Baseball (plus in this same arena, collecting autographs from sports players on baseballs or similar souvenirs.)

Whatever the goal, whatever you choose the objective remains the same, find something you enjoy and give your mind the relief it needs. Be sure to choose an activity that you love, this will ensure that you do it often and enjoy the gratification you derive form it.

CREATE YOUR ENVIRONMENT

Some individuals find it hard to think of themselves as a professional decorator but decorating for relaxation is simple. It just takes dropping a few items in each room to turn it into an oasis of calm relaxation. Your home is your escape from the world, somewhere that you can hide away and re-gain your strengths and rejuvenate your mind. Below are some tips that will stimulate your thoughts for stress-less decorating ideas. These ideas only focus on items that may be added to a room that would achieve a calm and relaxing effect.

Decorating for relaxation room by room.

Kitchen – Light and Nature should be the focus.

Use verticals or mini blinds for easy opening and closing for sunlight and privacy.

Place plants or a small garden of home grown herbs, in front of or by the window.

Install an under counter radio/CD player to listen to music while working in the kitchen.

Place a pot on the stove with the heating element on simmer. Place a couple of cinnamon sticks or cloves for a fragrant relaxing effect. You can also purchase liquid potpourri to use in the same manner.

Dining Room – Focus should be placed on table settings and centerpiece.

Flowers, Candles, and/or Incense make a great arrangement for centerpieces.

Placemats at each setting with napkins and rings create a welcoming feeling to friends and family

Plug-in diffusers save space in place of candles and still have a choice of relaxing aromas.

Living Room – Focus should be placed on relaxing entertainment.

A water fountain offset in a corner or on a table top can give you the ambiance and sounds of nature, which automatically queues our bodies to relax.

If you are not successful at keeping live plants healthy, try artificial trees set strategically to bring a feeling of nature to the inside of your home.

A fireplace can add atmosphere and warmth for family fun and gatherings, as well as comfort and romance for those nights of spending time with that someone special.

These are available in electric or Gel styles for the effects of a real fireplace. They give off heat and have screens for child and animal protection.

Decorating with candles is always beneficial to the senses of sight and smell. If children or animals prohibit this, try reed diffusers (still place these up high so they are not accidentally ingested or come in direct contact with skin).

There are also the battery operated votive candles now which deliver atmosphere without the danger of fire.

Bathroom – Focus on tranquil and comfort sensations.

Place small bottles of lavender lotions on the counter for easy access.

Reed diffusers or candles can be used for relaxing, while taking a bath.

Use a small shelf to hold lavender bath salts, bath oils, potpourri, and color coordinated washcloths rolled and tied with a ribbon.

 In a shower or bath stall you can add a water proof radio tuned to a relaxing station.

Adult Bedroom – focus should be on body relaxation and comfort.

Place a CD player with speakers on the bedside table. This player should have a headphone adaptor to plug in a speaker pillow for perfectly dreamy nights.

Depending on your preference, there are also sound therapy machines.

In a separate drawer keep some essential oils for a relaxing massage along with an eye pillow to release the head and eye tensions.

Keep a reading bed lounger or wedge on hand for those nights when you want to curl up and read a book or view some television, if this is your choice of relaxation.

Candles are great to be used for both dim light and aroma.

Soft padded bed with fluffy but supportive pillows.

There are also some massage mats that you can lay flat on your bed and relax with the rolling motion of massage.

Patio or outside space – focus on nature and sounds.

Fountains are a natural relaxation tool, as well as the sensations of listening to wind chimes as they sway in the breeze.

Have some sort of comfortable seating or hammock to lie back in and enjoy a lazy day.

Outdoor fireplaces are great conversation pieces as well as being useful items to create great atmosphere, warmth, and gathering spots for family and friends to chat, while taking a well deserved break from the day's activities.

Your vehicle – focus for comfort.

Yes, your car counts as part of your living space. Comfort and relaxation avoids those feelings of urgency and frustration in traffic.

There are car air diffusers or travel diffusers available to keep the scents of aromatherapy active and relaxing your senses.

For cold weather or just plain comfort, try a heated car seat cushion with massage.

Always keep a notepad, pen, and plenty of soothing sound CD's in stock.

Added Suggestions - For those pampering supplies that keep you looking forward to the end of the day treats try using foot baths or foot massagers – body massager's - comfy slippers, hand mitts, and neck wraps.

CHAPTER 9
MORGAN AND ME
CLOSING POSITIVE QUOTES

What ever happened to Morgan?

Morgan was saved from self destruction more than once, due to the love she had for her son. She feels if not for this bond she may have followed through with thoughts of suicide due to her emotional instability. Her life went from one extreme to the other and her emotions followed. The majority of her behavior through the years she was able to conceal from people she knew, since she would never allow that closeness of a friend and she would never depend on anyone other than herself. She built a world where she was the only one she would trust.

She reached a point in her life where through continued education, she understood that something was wrong with her thought patterns and she knew this had worsened over the years. As she gained strength through many self help books and distanced herself from her past, she applied many changes in her life. Although she was making progress, she still understood she needed to see a therapist to help her unravel buried emotions and resolve the destructive thought patterns.

Morgan reflects on a therapy session, "This is where I was taught to use meditations such as 'The Child Within' which, I altered for myself and renamed. I love this meditation even to this day. I still use it when I want to retreat and gather strength."

This is why expressive therapies come in so handy for a means of expression. Additionally, this is yet another example of why seeking the help of a psychiatrist is so important. It expands your knowledge of how to cope with your emotions and gives you a controlled environment to express your thoughts, as well as yields a diagnosis to any larger mental disorders you may need to deal with.

Morgan found after extensive research for herself, that her mother's past actions were displays of mental disorders that had trickled down from generations. Morgan's aunt was placed in an institution at a young age and that is where she spent the remainder of her days. Although Morgan's mother would never consent to receiving help, at least she had learned to understand why her mother acted the way she did. This also allowed her to tolerate her mother's continuous behavior and gave her more patience when speaking and having interactions with her mother. Morgan was able to conquer acceptance and forgiveness which helped with their relationship and permitted her to move forward in her own life.

She regrets that her son experienced a lot of her difficulties. They have always remained close and she hopes with his knowledge of hereditary disorders and mental complications that she experienced, that he will not only be able to identify and seek help if he should ever need to in the future but that he has gained an acceptance and understanding required so that nothing will ever stand in the way of their relationship, trust, and love for each other.

Morgan took the most difficult roads to find the stability that she needed to create a balance in her life because she did not trust confiding in anyone and has since dedicated her life to helping others to avoid this trap.

Morgan admits, "I have been really fortunate over the years, individuals who new me through my employment have always seen a spark in me that I never saw, they pushed me to keep moving forward. My mother pitted my sister and I against each other for about ten years before we caught on to what was truly happening. Then when we did start speaking to each other and comparing stories everything unraveled and we have since sworn to never let anything come between us again in our lives. I don't for one second, believe that my mother meant to intentionally hurt us ever but she was struggling with her own demons. I'll never really understand it but it seemed that she kept us apart so that she could have one hundred percent of the benefits and attention, that you could imagine two separate daughters could give. For the last nineteen years or so, my sister and I have been very close and I am particularly glad to have one other person in my life who visually and emotionally understands my battles."

"I started believing somewhere around the age of thirteen that I was being challenged by all of these trials so that I could help others confront their demons and find their way in life – I have never doubted this belief. I not only try to help people through every day living but have written two books in my endeavor's to widen the attempts in reaching the greater population. The first book is titled, *Cobwebs of the Mind – How to take Control of Stress* and the second book is the one you are now reading, *Creating Balance in a World of Stress*. I hope to continue to teach stress reduction and educate on the value of positive thinking and the importance of perception."

"Hi, my true name is Susan, the writer of this book and if you hadn't figured that out until now, then I succeeded in my attempt to use Morgan to describe some highlights of my life that corresponded with the points in this book. I intentionally brought Morgan to life for the purpose of a real life scenario and to draw personal interest to a character that many can relate to on some level. I guess the point I truly wanted to make was, that no matter how you feel today or what has transpired in your past, there is always hope for tomorrow if you are willing to learn and confront your fears, change your perceptions, bring balance into your life and grow into who you were meant to be. Remember...."

> *"Change your thoughts and you change your world"*
> *-Norman Vincent Peale*

Take the challenge today to start living your life by shifting the negative thought process to positive. Dwell on the compliments and learn from the criticisms. Let others see the light shine through your eyes. Discovering your fears and weaknesses will help you to overcome them and concentrate on your strengths and passions. Changing your thought pattern to positive thinking, defeating the stress that imprisons you, and learning physical fitness and proper nutrition for a balanced mind and body connection will stabilize your well-being and bring you the inner peace that you search for.

Take time for yourself to stop and relax, reflect, plan, and regain perspective over your life. Identify your negative behaviors and take the necessary steps to correct these self-limiting actions. Release the bonds that hold you powerless to control your own life. Triumph over stress and your ability to eradicate fear and negativity from your life. I hope you have realized how unbelievably strong you are and the importance of sharing what you have to offer with the rest of the world.

Live at peace and in harmony with the life that surrounds you. Once established, you will have the ability to spread your knowledge to help others create balance in there lives. There is no better gift to offer than to celebrate life as it was meant to be celebrated. Positive thinking may be one of those hurdles you have to work your way over but the benefits are enormous not only to you, but to every life that you touch on your journey.

I may never get to cross your path and hear of your accomplishments. I do however, believe you will find what you are searching for and I know that whatever you choose to do, you will somehow positively impact my life. Thank you in advance for sharing your gifts and the blessings that God intended for you to share.

Things I have learned through the years.

"Your thoughts express who you are, so if you are not who you want to be, you'll need to change your way of thinking."

"Fear is your own perception – that can be changed."

"Don't get fixated on the door that closed, look for the door that opened and choose to follow the paths that appear in front of you, they have been placed there for a reason."

"Not forgiving someone is allowing them to drain your energy. Forgive, learn from it, and let it go."

"Don't let Negativity enter your heart, for it breeds more negativity."

"There is positive and negative in any situation. Choose to view the positive."

"There will always be cloudy days when things seem to never go right, without these we would never learn and grow, we would just survive. Remember- the sun will be back to warm you."

"If you quit, you will never get the chance to know what might have been."

"Each year that arrives holds magnificent opportunities, keep focused on the positive in all that you do so that you don't blind yourself to these occasions."

"Don't view life in black and white, God gave us colors for our enjoyment."

"You have many talents - choose one that is a true passion and follow where it leads."

"Never let a day go by as a blur in front of your eyes – live and take the time to feel each moment as it passes, this is your life."

"Positive thoughts will yield positive results. Positive results will yield happiness."

"Babies see in amusement-children see in wonder. As an adult never lose sight of your inner child or you will lose these special qualities."

"A positive attitude is a stress free attitude."

"Positive people are like magnets, individuals are drawn to their optimism."

"Happiness is not hard to find, it is all around you if you choose to open your eyes and be thankful."

"Accepting change is a matter of perception. Think of only the positive attributes and change will come easier."

"The most important things in life are cost free and there for the taking. Laughs, smiles, hugs, support, friendship, family, compliments…"

"Mother Nature gives you a world of things to be thankful for."

"If you should ever trip, simply move the obstacle to the side and keep focused on your goal."

"When you are in a long, cold, dark tunnel---turn on the light. Sometimes we just don't look for the obvious."

"If you want to be an angel when you die, you'll need to practice while you live."

"Just as fall strips the trees to prepare for new growth, the snow cleanses the ground, and spring brings fresh flowers, everything and everyone has the ability to clean the slate and start anew."

"Prepare for the best, you would hate to be caught off guard."

"Stress is only bad if you let it dictate your life rather than motivate it."

"Life is fragile so pamper yourself with care."

"Nothing can have any more importance than what you place on it."

"Time is precious but it's nice to take the watch off and just live."

"Positive anticipation is good for the soul, it gives us the excitement and enthusiasm and a thirst for more."

"Never discount another's knowledge, when you can use it to build on. Suggestions open new possibilities."

"Altering your perception will change your direction."

"We all face many choices a day. You will always be in control of your own actions and reactions. If you think of someone else before you act and consider someone else before you react, you're sure to make the right choices."

"Positive thinking can remove obstacles and open the doors for you to walk through."

"Start to think positive today and watch for the results tomorrow!"

"Don't try to win someone else's approval, listen to the voice that guides you. Will that be the voice of man or the voice of God?"

"Being positive means there's no need to be boastful to draw attention to yourself since the light will always shine in your direction."

"Accept that everyone is different – some may only be able to concentrate on one thing at a time, while others thrive on multiple activities. Understand that others are also on a predestined path and don't ask or expect anything that is not freely given."

"You will always find fault in yourself if you look but you have been created with many talents and attractions. Focus and build on your strong attributes."

"Build bridges that can be crossed, not walls that create barriers."

"Be a blessing by making footprints for others to follow."

"Pursue your existence with excitement, enthusiasm, and passion and be thankful for each new day that arrives."

"Laughter is positive energy that is contagious. Transmit this disease in abundance."

"Maintaining a positive attitude means reenergizing your mind, body, and spirit daily to preserve the inner peace and beauty that you have established. Never neglect your inner health, for this shines the light that leads your way."

"The meaning of life is just thoughts away when you choose to discover it."

"Music and laughter should be prescribed on a daily basis. This would add years to your life."

"Self improvement will always be your goal since perfection will never surface."

"Progress is changing for the better and never wavering from your journey."

"Reflect on your younger years but never stop moving forward and creating new memories."

"Your mind simply processes what you see it's your heart that makes it worth seeing."

"Nobody will think exactly like you, cherish the ones you love and blind yourself to the differences."

"Happiness is found in those small moments that you may take for granted."

"Curiosity sparks imagination, imagination sparks growth, growth sparks curiosity. ~ Be curious."

"We envy pets for what they have, unconditional love, curiosity, and the wonder of how a small balled up piece of paper can keep them content for hours on end."

"It's the simple things in life that matter, yet we continue to try to complicate them."

"We never really fail at anything since we always take away more knowledge than we started with."

"Your imagination can take you anywhere you would like to be, so take vacations daily."

"Be thankful for difficult times, they give you challenges to exercise your positive thinking."

"Being a positive person does not come naturally when there is so much negativity in the world today. It's to your advantage to be positive so that you will stand out and be recognized."

"You can never fail if you live each day to please God rather than man."

"Find and focus on a hobby and there you will find your peace and tranquility and most of all therapy."

"Surround yourself only with items that make you smile. These are the things in your heart that are most important to you and as a result will keep your stress level low and your relaxation level high."

Susan J. Del Gatto

"When the day comes to a close be sure you don't end it with any regrets."

Thoughts by Susan J. Del Gatto

I hope at the end of every day your mind grows mentally and physically stronger

and your body grows mentally and physically more relaxed

Stress – It's all About Balance and Control

Happiness Always, Susan

Bibliography

Alise, C. [2009] 'About Sleeping Pills' [Online] Available from: http://www. ehow.com/about_4596295_sleeping-pills.html [Accessed February 21, 2009]

Bourne, Edmund, J. (2001) Beyond Anxiety & Phobia - New Harbinger Publications pg 43, 233, 226, 227

Bradshaw, John (1988) [a] Healing the Shame that Binds You – Health Communications, Inc. pg 51, 142, 164, 165, 176, 191

Bradshaw, John (1988) [b] The Family – Health Communications, Inc. Pg 5, 88, 94

Castleman, Michael (2000) Blended Medicine, Yoga, Rodale publishing, pg 43, 296, 299

Cernaj, & Kolster – Balance- Stress-free and Relaxed in Minutes1999, English edition, Sing Cheong Printing Co. Ltd., Hong Kong Pg 26

Giacobello, John (2000) Anxiety and Panic Attacks - Rosen publishing Group pg 14

HART-Empire, The 26 Aug, 2007- Stress and Alcohol [Online] Available from: http://stress.battlingforhealth.com/2007/08/stress-and-alcohol/ [Accessed February 21, 2009]

Health Care Center, The - Anger Management and Stress: Manage Your Anger To Reduce Stress [Online] Available from: http://www. thehealthcarecenter.com/anger_management_and_stress.html [Accessed December 11, 2008]

Heider, Fritz (1959) On Perception and Event Structure, and the Psychological Environment: Selected Papers, Vol. 1 - International Universities Press

Jacobson, Edmond (1976) You Must Relax 5th edition – McGraw-Hill Book Company, Pg 86, 90, 251

Jampolsky, Gerald (1979) Love Is Letting Go Of Fear – Ten Speed Press,. pg 77-78, 65, 53

Kinder, Melvyn (1990) Going Nowhere Fast – Prentice Hall Press pg 107, 278

Knaus, William (1994) Change your life now – John Wiley & Sons,Inc. 114-115, 118, 166, 148, 161

Kunz, Barbara & Kevin (2006) hand reflexology – Dorling Kindersley Limited pg 24

Market Wire - "Harvard Eye Associates Expert Warns Against Sun Damage to the Eyes" [Online] Available from: http://findarticles.com/p/articles/mi_pwwi/is_200805/ai_n25442483 [Accessed August 2, 2008]

Mayo Clinic Staff (2006) - Stress symptoms and signs Prompt recognition is crucial [Online] Available from: http://www.mayoclinic.com/health/stress-symptoms/SR00008

Mondimore, Francis Mark (2006) Bipolar Disorder – Johns Hopkins Press pg 51, 149

Mornhinweg, Gail - Journal of Holistic Nursing, University of Louisville, Music for Sleep Disturbance

Myer, Joyce (1995) Battlefield of the Mind – Harrison House, Inc. pg 41

National Acupuncture and Oriental Medicine Alliance - Quick Facts About Acupuncture and Oriental Medicine in the US [Online] Available from: http://www.acuall.org/gen.html [Accessed February 16, 2009]

Perry, Susan (2006) Good Health Handbook, Key Elements of a Healthy Lifestyle – National Health & Wellness Club, pg 24

Streeter, Michael (2004) Hypnosis-Secrets of the Mind – Barron's Educational Series, Inc. pg 51, 76

Stuart, Catherine (2007) Massage and aromatherapy – National Book Network pg 100, 369

Toy, Fiona (2002) Auras and Chakras – Lansdowne Publishing Pty Ltd. pg 54

Washington Post - Nancy Trejos, Staff Writer - All-Consuming Problem [Online] Available from: http://www.washingtonpost.com/wp-dyn/content/article/2008/06/28/AR2008062800229.html?hpid=moreheadlines [Accessed February 21, 2009]

Williamson, Marianne (1992) Return To Love – Harper Collins Publishers Pg 29, 36, 53-54

ABOUT THE AUTHOR

Susan J. Del Gatto is the author of Cobwebs of the Mind – How to Take Control of Stress and owner-operator of www.abc-stress.com. She holds a degree in social work and has over thirty years of professional experience. She currently resides in Florida.

INDEX

6 ways that we choose to reduce stress that may cause even more stress and damage to our health.